VERTICAL CHURCH

LifeWay Press ®
Nashville, Tennessee

Published by LifeWay Press®
© 2012 James MacDonald

No part of this book may be reproduced or transmitted in any form or by any means, electronic or mechanical, including photocopying and recording, or by any information storage or retrieval system, except as may be expressly permitted in writing by the publisher. Requests for permission should be addressed in writing to LifeWay Press®; One LifeWay Plaza; Nashville, TN 37234-0152.

ISBN 978-1-4158-7430-1
Item 005522647

Dewey decimal classification: 262.7
Subject headings: CHURCH \ GOD \ PRAISE OF GOD

Unless indicated otherwise, all Scripture quotations are taken from The Holy Bible, English Standard Version, copyright © 2000, 2001 by Crossway Bibles, a division of Good News Publishers. Scripture quotations marked NKJV are taken from the New King James Version. Copyright © 1979, 1980, 1982, Thomas Nelson Inc. Publishers. Scripture quotation marked NIV is taken from the Holy Bible, New International Version. copyright © 1973, 1978, 1984 by International Bible Society.

To order additional copies of this resource, write to LifeWay Church Resources Customer Service; One LifeWay Plaza; Nashville, TN 37234-0113; fax (615) 251-5933; phone toll free (800) 458-2772; order online at www.lifeway.com; e-mail orderentry@lifeway.com; or visit the LifeWay Christian Store serving you.

Printed in the United States of America

Adult Ministry Publishing
LifeWay Church Resources
One LifeWay Plaza
Nashville, TN 37234-0152

CONTENTS

THE AUTHOR

James MacDonald has committed his life to the unapologetic proclamation of God's Word. He is the founding senior pastor of Harvest Bible Chapel, one of the fastest-growing churches in the Chicago area, reaching more than 13,000 lives each weekend. Through James's leadership and by God's grace, a church-planting ministry was formed in 2002, Harvest Bible Fellowship, which has planted more than 73 churches across North America and around the world.

James also teaches on *Walk in the Word,* a daily radio broadcast committed to igniting passion in the people of God through the proclamation of truth.

Born in London, Ontario, Canada, James received his master's degree from Trinity Evangelical Divinity School in Deerfield, Illinois, and his doctorate from Phoenix Seminary. He and his wife, Kathy, have three adult children and reside in Chicago.

For more information about James and these ministries, visit *www.harvestbible.org* or *www.jamesmacdonald.com.*

Other books and small-group studies by James MacDonald:
> *Always True: God's Promises When Life Is Hard* small-group study (LifeWay Press, 2011)
> *Always True: God's Five Promises for When Life Is Hard* (Moody Publishers, 2011)
> *Downpour: He Will Come to Us like the Rain* small-group study (LifeWay Press, 2006)
> *Downpour: He Will Come to Us like the Rain* (B&H Publishing Group, 2006)
> *God Wrote a Book* (Crossway Books, 2002)
> *Gripped by the Greatness of God* small-group study (LifeWay Press, 2005)
> *Gripped by the Greatness of God* (Moody Publishers, 2005)
> *Have the Funeral* small-group study (LifeWay Press, 2011)
> *I Really Want to Change … So, Help Me God* (Moody Publishers, 2000)
> *Lord, Change Me* (Moody Publishers, 2012)
> *Lord, Change My Attitude* small-group study (LifeWay Press, 2008)
> *Lord, Change My Attitude … Before It's Too Late* (Moody Publishers, 2001)
> *Seven Words to Change Your Family* (Moody Publishers, 2001)
> *When Life Is Hard* small-group study (LifeWay Press, 2010)
> *When Life Is Hard* (Moody Publishers, 2010)
> *Vertical Church* (David C Cook, 2012)

Visit *www.lifeway.com/jamesmacdonald* for information about James MacDonald resources published by LifeWay.

INTRODUCTION

Your experiences with God, both individually and corporately, can be window-rattling, earth-shattering, life-altering encounters with the revealed glory of the Creator of the universe. That's the primary focus of this study, and that's my prayer for you and the other members of your church.

Are you ready to dive in?

This study is neatly divided into two halves. The first four weeks are a biblical exploration of humanity's universal longing to experience God's glory and the role of the church as God's designated contact point with His people. These sessions are designed to make the doctrinal case for shifting our focus from inadequate horizontal models of church to God's design for vertical church.

Having established the priority of vertical church and the consequence of its neglect, in the second half of this study we'll explore the *how* of vertical church. We'll examine the four pillars of vertical church in great detail and learn about vital practices that invite God to show His glory in manifest ways.

The four pillars of vertical church are:
> **Unashamed adoration**
> **Unapologetic preaching**
> **Unafraid witness**
> **Unceasing prayer**

Church was never intended to be a place where we serve God to the exclusion of meeting with Him. The Christian life should involve so much more than horizontal relationships and a weak, intellectual assent that God is real and may or may not have a place in the world. We can't survive spiritually without a corporate connection in heart, soul, mind, and strength with the One who made us. That's what I mean by *vertical*. A vertical focus positions a church to experience God's presence and to show the world what it means to serve a God of awe-inspiring power and glory.

How to Get the Most from This Study

1. **Attend each group experience.**
> **Watch the DVD teaching.**
> **Participate in the group discussions.**

2. **Complete the content in this workbook.**
> **Read the daily lessons.**
> **Complete the learning activities.**
> **Memorize each week's suggested memory verse.**
> **Watch for window-rattling, earth-shattering, life-altering encounters with God's revealed glory and manifest presence.**

A UNIVERSAL LONGING

TRANSCENDENCE

WEEK ONE

START

Welcome to this small-group discussion of *Vertical Church.*

To facilitate introductions and introduce the theme of *Vertical Church,* form a line based on height—the tallest person in the group at the back and the shortest person in the front. Then return to your seats to discuss the remaining questions.

When you hear the term *vertical,* what words or images come to mind? Why?

In your opinion, what do people long to experience in life? What are we all looking for?

Where do people typically turn to fulfill those longings?

To prepare to view the DVD segment, read these verses aloud.

> *My thoughts are not your thoughts,*
> *neither are your ways my ways, declares the LORD.*
> *For as the heavens are higher than the earth,*
> *so are my ways higher than your ways*
> *and my thoughts than your thoughts.*
> Isaiah 55:8-9

WATCH

Complete the viewer guide below as you watch DVD session 1.

There is a universal longing in every _____ _____.

God has made you a living _____.

Every person has in their heart a longing for something _____ of and _____ than themselves.

We are all the _____.

The universal longing is for _____.

Humans have a deep and abiding sense of something that _____ our immediate situation.

There is something not only similar but universally _____ about every human being from every culture throughout history.

Eternity means _____.

TRANSCENDENCE
1. Transcending _____ or _____ human experience
2. Existing apart from and not subject to the limitations of the _____ universe

Maybe the greatest rationality of all is the recognition that rationality itself is _____ as a way of knowing.

EXPERIENCING TRANSCENDENCE
1. When something wise reveals my small amount of _____
2. When something big reveals my small amount of _____
3. When something infinite reminds me that I am _____

We long for _____ but can't find it.

God created our longing for transcendence so that we would _____ Him.

IMPLICATIONS
1. _____ feels the pain of God's absence until they find Him.
2. _____ by others to fill the void will end in futility and should provoke compassion in us.
3. _____ expended to reach people should focus on God and the gospel.

VIDEO SESSIONS AVAILABLE FOR PURCHASE AT **WWW.LIFEWAY.COM/VERTICALCHURCH**

RESPOND

Discuss the DVD segment with your group, using the questions below.

> What did you like most about the DVD segment? Why?

> What's your reaction to this statement? "Every person has in their heart a longing for something outside of and greater than themselves."

> As a group, work to come up with a one-sentence definition of *transcendence*.

> In what ways have you experienced a longing for eternity and transcendence?

> In what ways can you see those longings reflected in our culture? Think about advertising, the entertainment industry, the news, and so on.

> What's your reaction to this statement? "Any discussion or understanding of the church has to begin with the knowledge that it is our mission to help as many people as possible find what their heart is looking for."

> How have you participated in this foundational aspect of the church's mission? How would you like to participate more fully?

APPLICATION

Throughout this week keep an eye open for moments when you experience the bigness and transcendence of God. Write those moments down and be prepared to talk about them at the beginning of next week's discussion.

SCRIPTURE MEMORY FOR THIS WEEK
He has made everything beautiful in its time. Also, he
has put eternity into man's heart, yet so that he cannot find
out what God has done from the beginning to the end.
Ecclesiastes 3:11

READ WEEK 1 AND COMPLETE THE ACTIVITIES BEFORE THE NEXT GROUP EXPERIENCE.

WEEK 1

"He has made everything beautiful in its time. Also, he has put eternity into man's heart, yet so that he cannot find out what God has done from the beginning to the end."

Ecclesiastes 3:11

SAY IT IN A SENTENCE >

Deep in the soul of every human being is a longing for transcendence that is created by God Himself.

A FRESH ENCOUNTER >

For me it all began one summer in upstate New York. I understand now that sending me to camp—a rebellious, stubborn teen—must have been welcome relief to my parents and that they must have been floored when I rushed into the kitchen 10 days later and shattered their peace with this pronouncement: "Mom and Dad, I found God!"

It was the language of experience, although subsequent good theology heightened my appreciation of the grace that actually *found me*. It could have been a mere flash in the pan, and it might have faded by Labor Day weekend of 1976. But it didn't.

Even though I tried to escape, the Lord continued His pursuit of my stubborn heart, and He continues it today. Was I saved that summer, or did He bring me back again to the profession I had made as a 7-year-old boy beside my mother's bed on a cold February night 10 years earlier? I don't know.

But I do know this about that summer: I relished the heartfelt worship in a room called the Tabernacle, packed to the rafters with high-school students. I heard the passionate preaching of Christ and His Word in a way that truly engaged my heart. I experienced the loving interaction of authentic Christians who cared in a way that didn't seem contrived. And I bene-fited from the fervent prayers offered spontaneously outside the dining hall or on the path back to my cabin.

There in the beauty and majesty of the Adirondack Mountains, beside the deep blue of Schroon Lake, New York, God power-fully burst into my soul. And since that day I've never been satisfied with anything less.

I hope you've had that kind of experience in the past. More importantly, I hope you desperately desire that kind of experi-ence both now and in the future, because that's what we're going to focus on this week.

Day 1 /

ETERNITY

TODAY'S SCRIPTURE FOCUS >

"He has made everything beautiful in its time. Also, he has put eternity into man's heart, yet so that he cannot find out what God has done from the beginning to the end." Ecclesiastes 3:11

There's a *universal* longing in the hearts of human beings. And by universal I mean it's everywhere. Every person on the face of the globe experiences this longing in a real and intense way. Every person in your family has this longing—every person at work, every person in your neighborhood, and every person in the town or city where you live.

In addition to being universal, this longing is also vital. It's critical. This searching, deep in our souls, is a hunger that food can never feed, clothing can never cover, and shelter can never warm. At times it becomes a ravenous longing that demands satisfaction beyond our accomplishments and accumulations. Billionaires around the globe are miserable because this longing goes unfulfilled. At the other end of the spectrum are single moms with hungry children in mud huts who overflow with joy because they've found what they long for.

What are some experiences or realities that most people long for?

Write down a specific human longing that has recently captured your attention.

WE LONG FOR ETERNITY

The universal longing at the core of every human heart is for eternity. We yearn for something lasting. Even as we hustle through busy days filled with families and jobs and traffic and hobbies and entertainment and rest, there's a whisper in the back of our minds that pulls us toward something deeper and infinitely more significant: eternity.

What first comes to mind when you hear the word *eternity*?

Define _eternity_ in your own words.

When most people think about eternity, they think in terms of eternal life. And the Scriptures certainly have a lot to say about that subject.

Read the following verses. What does each contribute to your understanding of eternity and eternal life?

John 3:14-16

John 5:19-24

John 5:37-40

John 12:24-25

Eternity is a reality we must all consider because we will all be somewhere for eternity. Eternal life is a big part of the universal longing we all experience.

At the same time, we need to understand that eternity is more than a future destination. It's not distant and out there. Rather, eternity is present with us now. That's what Solomon was talking about in Today's Scripture Focus: "[God] has put eternity into man's heart" (Eccl. 3:11).

What do you think this verse means when it says God "has put eternity into man's heart"?

How have you experienced a longing for eternity?

Look at what Jesus said in John 5:24: "Truly, truly, I say to you, whoever hears my word and believes him who sent me has eternal life. He does not come into judgment, but has passed from death to life." Notice Jesus didn't say, "Whoever hears my word and believes him who sent me _will have_ eternal life." He said "has." He spoke in the present tense. The same is true of the second half of the verse. Jesus didn't say a person who follows Him "_will pass_ from death to life." He said such a person "_has passed_ from death to life." Jesus used the past tense because it's already happened.

If you've been captured by the grace of God and received the salvation He's offered, you've already passed from death to life. You've received eternal life, and you're living in the reality of eternity.

What's your reaction to the previous statements? Why?

How does it change your definition of *eternity* to see it as a present reality rather than a future destination?

How does understanding eternity as a present reality affect your view of everyday life?

We all long for eternity, and for those who follow Jesus, eternity is a present reality. Here's something else we need to understand: this longing for eternity didn't come about by accident. It's a gift from God. It's part of God's design for human beings.

Genesis 2:7 records the moment when we received that gift: "The Lord God formed the man of dust from the ground and breathed into his nostrils the breath of life, and the man became a living creature." The Hebrew word translated "breath of life" is *ruach.* It's what the Creator breathed into humanity that distinguishes us from all other living things. It's why you know deep inside that you're not an animal and didn't come from one.

Rather, humans are unique from all other forms of life on this planet because we're created as spiritual beings. We're a divinely blended mix of flesh and soul, body and spirit. And in the center of each of us is a hunger for something that the experiences of this planet cannot satisfy—a quest for eternity.

What are some ways people express their hunger for eternity?

What are some ways you personally experience and express that hunger?

ETERNITY IS VERTICAL

Let's conduct a little experiment. I want you to look at something. You don't have to look at something big or impressive; you don't even have to look at something interesting. Just spend a few seconds looking at something around you and then write down what you see. Go ahead.

What did you look at?

Here's the next part of the experiment. Which direction did you look? Whatever your eyes focused on for those few seconds, did you look up to see it? Did you look down? Did your eyes stay on a horizontal plane?

Which direction did you look?

I'm guessing you didn't look up. That's because for human beings, looking up is the least natural thing we do. Try looking up for a few moments and see if you don't find it a lot easier to look down—to gaze in front of you rather than to throw your head back and look skyward.

As human beings, we have a horizontal focus. We live on earth; we're flatlanders. That means we constantly try to bring things down to our level—and not just in terms of what we see.

> **Read Genesis 3:1-13. What did Adam and Eve gain in this passage?**

> **What did they lose?**

The story of the fall is a classic example of our human propensity toward horizontal thinking. Adam and Eve enjoyed an amazingly intimate relationship with God. This connection was vertical. Adam and Eve were created beings, but they were uniquely connected with the Creator; they had a vertical relationship with God. In Genesis 3, however, their focus became primarily horizontal. They saw the snake. They saw the fruit. They understood the fruit would taste good, and it might even make them smarter. Their sin resulted when their horizontal focus overpowered their vertical relationship with God.

> **Look again at Genesis 3:1-13. Write down the elements of the story that are horizontal.**

> **Write down the elements of the story that are vertical.**

All of us make the same mistake Adam and Eve made. We're sinful people, so we specialize in displacing the vertical with the horizontal.

The bad news is that we'll never be satisfied by such a substitution. We were created for a vertical relationship with God. That's the only reality that can satisfy the universal longing we all feel—that hunger for eternity we all experience.

The good news is that we don't have to settle for the horizontal offerings of this world. God continually offers us opportunities to fulfill our longing for eternity by maintaining a vertical focus on Him. That's what we'll explore the rest of this week.

ETERNITY MEANS TRANSCENDENCE

TODAY'S SCRIPTURE FOCUS >

"My thoughts are not your thoughts,

neither are your ways my ways, declares the LORD.

For as the heavens are higher than the earth,

so are my ways higher than your ways

and my thoughts than your thoughts." Isaiah 55:8-9

So far we've talked about the universal longing at the heart of the human experience. This longing is not just similar but identical for every human being from every culture throughout history. The access points or expressions of that longing may vary from culture to culture, but the underlying vacuum in the center of every soul is a manufacturer's specification from God Himself.

In other words, God has placed eternity in our hearts (see Eccl. 3:11), and we long to experience it.

But *eternity* is a general term. It's a word people use to describe what they haven't fully experienced. So as we go forward in this study, let's take the idea of what we're created to long for and move it a little closer to the flame. Let's talk about transcendence.

What first comes to mind when you hear the word *transcendence*?

Define *transcendence* in your own words.

DEFINITIONS

The dictionary doesn't give us a lot of help in defining *transcendence*. Here's what it says: "The action or fact of transcending, surmounting, or rising above ... the attribute of being above and independent of the universe."[1]

Wayne Gruden helps us put some meat on the bones of this essential longing: "The term often used to say that God is much greater than creation is the word *transcendent*. Very simply, this means that God is far 'above' the creation in the sense that he is greater than the creation and he is independent of it."[2]

That's a key phrase: "far above." When something is transcendent, it's on a vastly different level from the normal, commonplace elements of everyday life. To be transcendent means to be lifted far above everything else.

Let's take a moment to get a little hands-on with this concept of transcendence. Wherever you are right now, look around and write down five things you see. Don't write down things that are similar, though. Find something big, something little, something valuable, something worthless, and something that's special to you personally.

Write down what you see.

Something big:

Something little:

Something valuable:

Something worthless:

Something special:

Now think of five things you know—five concepts you're familiar with and understand. For example, "I love my wife." It can be a mathematical formula, a philosophical statement, a tip for cooking steak, or anything else you know and comprehend.

Write down what you know.

1.

2.

3.

4.

5.

Here's the point. Each thing you wrote down is an example of something that's *not* transcendent, and each thing you wrote down represents a whole world of objects and ideas that are *not* transcendent. If you can see something or put your fingers on it, it isn't transcendent. If you can understand an idea or a concept—if you can wrap your brain around it and feel that you fully comprehend what's going on— then it's not transcendent.

To be transcendent means to be far above the normal, understandable objects and ideas around us in the world. Are you tracking with me on the concept of transcendence? It's an important foundation for what we're going to look at next.

GOD IS TRANSCENDENT

So often we talk about God as if we understand Him. We rattle off theological definitions or platitudes, and we act as if we've got our minds firmly wrapped around all God is and everything He does.

That's not the case. No matter how much you know, God is transcendent. He is far above anything we could ever hope to touch or comprehend. In his book *The Knowledge of the Holy*, A. W. Tozer warned us about overreaching in our understanding of God:

> We must not think of God as highest in an ascending order of beings,
> starting with the single cell and going on up from the fish to the bird
> to the animal to man to angel to cherub to God. This would be to grant
> God eminence, even pre-eminence, but that is not enough;
> we must grant Him transcendence in the fullest meaning of that word.[3]

In other words, God is wholly other; He breaks all the categories of being and knowing. God Himself made the same declaration in Today's Scripture Focus:

> **My thoughts are not your thoughts,
> neither are your ways my ways, declares the LORD.
> For as the heavens are higher than the earth,
> so are my ways higher than your ways
> and my thoughts than your thoughts.** Isaiah 55:8-9

Do you agree or disagree that we'll never be able to fully understand God? Why?

What aspects of God's character and activity in the world are we able to comprehend?

This reality of God's transcendence is why the authors of Scripture so often used language connected with height and distance when they wrote about Him. For example, David wrote in Psalm 8:1:

> *O LORD, our Lord,*
> *how majestic is your name in all the earth!*
> *You have set your glory above the heavens.*

What do the following verses express about God's transcendence?

Psalm 71:19

Psalm 89:13

Psalm 103:11

Transcendence is the best single word I've found to describe the infinite awesomeness of who God is and what He does throughout the universe. It also describes what's all too often missing from our lives—and from our churches.

Every human being experiences a longing to connect with eternity, to have an encounter with transcendence—which means every human being really has a longing for God.

OUR FUTILE SEARCH

TODAY'S SCRIPTURE FOCUS   >

"His invisible attributes, namely, his eternal power and divine nature, have been clearly perceived, ever since the creation of the world, in the things that have been made. So they are without excuse. For although they knew God, they did not honor him as God or give thanks to him, but they became futile in their thinking, and their foolish hearts were darkened. Claiming to be wise, they became fools, and exchanged the glory of the immortal God for images resembling mortal man and birds and animals and creeping things." Romans 1:20-23

There's never been a better time to search for something you need to find. If you need information on just about any subject, you need only hop online and use Google or Bing. If you're looking for a business or a residential address, you can use GPS technology. If you're looking for a person, chances are pretty good you'll find them on Facebook or LinkedIn.

Even with all the tools available today, however, most people on this planet are involved in a fruitless, futile search for fulfillment in their lives. They're frantically seeking a way to satisfy the longing for transcendence that God has planted within them. Sadly, their efforts come up empty because they're looking in the wrong place. They're searching horizontally rather than vertically.

Give examples of places people look for fulfillment in life.

Identify a product or service you've recently seen advertised that claimed to provide greater meaning or fulfillment in life.

This week we've been exploring the universal longing for eternity that is present in the hearts of all human beings. Every person who's ever lived has longed for transcendence, which means every person who's ever lived has searched for it in one way or another.

More than three thousand years ago, one of the wisest and richest men of all time conducted his own futile search for fulfillment. That man was Solomon, the ancient king of Israel, and he chronicled his journey in the timeless Book of Ecclesiastes.

SOLOMON'S SEARCH

If a human being ever strolled down every conceivable avenue of potential satisfaction without finding it, that person was Solomon. The Book of Ecclesiastes details Solomon's experimentation with every pleasure, from constructing a palace so opulent that it staggered world leaders to accumulating innumerable jewels and possessions. Solomon pursued advanced academic studies, sex with different women, and every other amusement he could think of. He explored every possible indulgence of the lifestyles of the rich and famous.

Here's what Solomon concluded after all his striving and searching and doing: "Vanity of vanities, says the Preacher, vanity of vanities! All is vanity. What does man gain by all the toil at which he toils under the sun?" (Eccl. 1:2-3). Solomon also wrote in Ecclesiastes 2, "I hated life, because what is done under the sun was grievous to me, for all is vanity and a striving after wind" (v. 17).

What's your reaction to Solomon's summary of his experiences? Why?

What situations or scenarios cause you to feel frustrated with life?

Have you seen any of the old "Merrie Melodies" cartoons featuring Wile E. Coyote and the Road Runner? In every episode the coyote is desperate to catch the Road Runner. He's starving, and his whole world is focused on finding and capturing the bird. He goes to incredible lengths to make it happen—running as hard as he can, donning elaborate disguises, even purchasing all kinds of gadgets and traps. But nothing works. No matter how hard he tries, the coyote winds up empty-handed before the credits roll.

Solomon had a lot in common with Wile E. Coyote. The king spent day after day pursuing every horizontal experience he could think of in an effort to fulfill his longing for transcendence. But nothing worked. Solomon discovered what so many fail to realize: history is a repetitive loop of personal futility, and every imaginable experience of the horizontal promises fulfillment it never truly gives.

What other figures in history are famous for struggling to find fulfillment in this life?

Take a moment to think of modern celebrities who have publicly destroyed themselves in an effort to find meaning in life. What are some common elements in their stories?

In Ecclesiastes 3 Solomon turned his expression of frustration on the God who made him, and he cried out, "He has made everything beautiful in its time. Also, he has put eternity into man's heart, yet so that he cannot find out what God has done from the beginning to the end" (v. 11).

This wasn't a positive statement from Solomon. This was a frustrated cry of anguish. Solomon had spent years and years searching for a way to find fulfillment through earthly experiences, and he was ultimately crushed by the realization that he couldn't do it. On his own he couldn't fashion any kind of happiness or satisfaction that would endure for more than a few moments.

Like Solomon, we can't fashion happiness for ourselves either. I was aware of Ecclesiastes 3:11 for many years before the second part of the verse caught my full attention: "… yet so that he cannot find out what God has done from the beginning to the end." If you're looking for an answer to the mystery of human misery, X marks the spot—Ecclesiastes 3:11b.

The implications of Solomon's statement are staggering: people are looking for the eternity God created them to long for, but they can't find it on their own. Like a hungry man outside a locked gourmet restaurant, we know satisfaction is near but can't get to the food. Like a blind man on the edge of the Grand Canyon, we feel the awesomeness close at hand but have no capacity to see it.

Searching for eternity doesn't lead to finding until God Himself intercepts our wandering pursuit.

How does God attempt to interrupt our wandering pursuit of fulfillment?

In the end Solomon rightly observed that fulfillment must come from a source outside ourselves and beyond this world: "There is nothing better for a person than that he should eat and drink and find enjoyment in his toil. This also, I saw, is from the hand of God, for apart from him who can eat or who can have enjoyment?" (Eccl. 2:24-25).

Do you get it? God made you the way you are, and He made me the same way. God designed us so that we can't find fulfillment or lasting enjoyment apart from eternity. The more frantically we try to satisfy our deepest longing by good and bad horizontal means, the more likely we are to miss God's vertical invitation to find fulfillment in Him.

OUR SEARCH

Collectively and individually, all of us are conducting the same search as Solomon. We're all looking to fulfill our longing for transcendence. Unfortunately, most people in modern society have taken the same path as Solomon, even if they don't realize it.

Some people try to fulfill their longing through achievement and success. They pour every ounce of energy into business strategies and making money. They get up early. They work late. They continually strive to beat down the competition and rise to new levels of accomplishment. Yet they aren't satisfied.

Others try to fulfill their longing through pleasures and vices, or perhaps they attempt to escape their longing altogether. They turn to sex. They turn to food. They turn to drugs and alcohol. They turn to anything that will distract them—even for a moment—from the ache that keeps pulsing deep in their souls. Yet they aren't satisfied.

Reread Today's Scripture Focus. In what other ways do people attempt to satisfy or escape their longing for fulfillment?

In what ways have you attempted to satisfy or escape that longing?

I hate to say it, but there are also a number of people who attempt to satisfy their longings through "good" things. Many parents selflessly empty themselves day after day in an effort to benefit their children, for example. Many people dedicate themselves to their spouses in ways that put romantic comedies to shame. There are even people who spend hours and hours serving at church because they feel that longing for eternity and want to experience relief.

List three additional "good" things Christians try to use as substitutes for transcendence.

All of those activities are good and helpful, but none of them will satisfy our longing for eternity without a vertical focus on our transcendent God. The very best thing you could ever do will have no impact in our world and bring no satisfaction to your soul if your focus is horizontal rather than vertical.

As a pastor, I see it every day. So many people are searching and searching and searching, but they never find what they're looking for because the eyes of their hearts are focused on the world rather than on God. They're looking horizontally.

Don't let that be you this week. Look up! Look for an encounter with the eternal, transcendent God, and you'll find the satisfaction you so desperately crave.

Take a moment to pray. Confess to God any futile ways you have tried to satisfy your longing for transcendence. Confess to Him that only He can fulfill your need. Ask Him to give you a vertical focus as you continue this study.

OUR MISTAKEN BELIEFS

TODAY'S SCRIPTURE FOCUS >

"The LORD answered Job out of the whirlwind and said:

'Dress for action like a man;

I will question you, and you make it known to me.

Will you even put me in the wrong?

Will you condemn me that you may be in the right?

Have you an arm like God,

and can you thunder with a voice like his?' " Job 40:6-9

Today I want to explore two foundational concepts influencing the lives and behaviors of most Americans, including American Christians. These are two of the primary roots that have supplied and supported the tree of evangelicalism throughout the past decade.

The first of these roots is philosophical; the second is theological. And the reason we need to talk about them is that these two foundational beliefs often work to push us away from our need for transcendence. They keep us focused on the horizontal experiences of life rather than on our vertical relationship with God.

We'll start with the philosophy.

TRANSCENDENCE VS. RATIONALISM

"Prove it." How many times have you heard those words? How many times have you spoken them? That common phrase succinctly illustrates the philosophical way of thinking known as rationalism.

At its core, rationalism teaches that we should base our entire perception of the universe on what can be known and understood. This worldview is founded on logic, reason, and the scientific method. Rationalism says if you can't quantify something, if you can't show it to me or provide evidence to prove it, it's not real—or at least it's not important enough to think about or pursue.

You can gain a practical understanding of the way rationalism works by answering the following questions.

What is 2 + 2?

How do you know gravity is real and at work in the world?

Who wrote *The Chronicles of Narnia?*

Each of those questions has a logical, testable answer. You can take two coins out of your pocket, add two more, and count the total to prove that 2 + 2 = 4. You know that gravity is real because when you jump in the air, you fall back down again. And you can prove that C. S. Lewis wrote *The Chronicles of Narnia* by digging through historical records and copyright claims.

So on one level, rationalism makes sense, right? Logic, reason, and testable hypotheses are valued in our society. However, there's a limit to what rationalism can explain. And you can get a sense of that limit by answering this next set of questions.

Who is the most famous person in the world?

How do you know you love your mother?

What are the exact time and date you will die?

Many questions simply can't be answered rationally because they go beyond our ability to test or think logically. So rationalism is a limited way of thinking.

Here's the main thing we need to understand: rationalism pushes us away from transcendence. If something is far above our experience and our ability to comprehend, rationalism refuses to acknowledge its existence or importance. In other words, a rationalistic worldview actively teaches us to deny the longing for eternity that's been planted in our hearts.

This is a problem for two reasons. First, rationalism impacts much of our everyday lives. We spend the vast majority of our time focusing on concepts or problems that can be reasoned out and logically understood. We have budgets, for example. We have to solve conflicts between our children or coworkers. We have lawns to mow, movies to watch, and meals to cook.

Given those experiences, we're regularly tempted to approach our relationship with God through the lens of rationalism rather than seek a vertical encounter with transcendence. And sadly, we regularly give in to that temptation, often without realizing it.

In what ways do you see rationalism working against transcendence in the world today?

What portions of your life are most influenced by a rationalistic way of thinking?

How has rationalism affected your relationship with God?

Second, rationalism can be a problem because it has a major impact on churches and their leaders. In a society where rationality has ruled for a long time, the church frequently fails to see that in forsaking the weekly pursuit of the transcendent, we've given up the only ground that was uniquely ours in this world. In attempting to make the church something that can attract and add value to secular mind-sets, we've turned our backs on our one true value proposition—transcendence.

In other words, the entity God created to communicate His transcendence has fallen far from its mission when it chooses instead to traffic what can be found on any street corner or at the local mall. You may ask, "But how has the church done that?" I've noticed at least four primary ways:

- By offering secularists what they find mildly interesting and calling it church
- By submitting to self-help sermons in which an encounter with God is not even on the agenda
- By letting the horizontal excellence of the performance stand in for vertical impact
- By substituting the surprise or shock of superficial entertainment for the supernatural presence of God

When we settle for a festival of felt needs at church, we fail to offer what God has charged us exclusively to give. We fail to facilitate what God has created people to need, and that is eternity—transcendence—the rare experience of something totally beyond ourselves.

Has rationalism influenced your experiences at church? If so, how?

What impact has rationalism had on the church as a whole in recent decades?

As individuals and churches, we must return to a vertical, transcendent relationship with God that regularly interrupts and alters the horizontal, rational elements of our everyday lives.

TRANSCENDENCE VS. IMMANENCE

Now let's turn to theology. Let's talk about immanence.

Many of us love to hear about the ways God loves us. We enjoy reading about His compassion, His care, and His mercy. Those aspects of God's character can be summed up in the word *immanence*—that He is close to us and wants us to be in a relationship with Him.

Now let me say this right off the bat: these immanent aspects of God's character are certainly real, and we can absolutely experience them. The Bible makes that clear.

Read the following passages of Scripture and write ways they contribute to your understanding of God's immanence.

Hebrews 4:14-16

Psalm 65:9-13

John 3:16-17

God is loving. He is merciful. He is caring and compassionate. And He wants to have a relationship with us. But we make a big mistake when we focus on those immanent aspects of God's character to the exclusion of His transcendence.

This is a mystery, but God is both immanent *and* eminent. He is close to us, yes, but He is also far above us. He is compassionate but also holy. He offers His love to us, but He also responds to our sin with wrath.

Read the following passages of Scripture and write ways they contribute to your understanding of God's transcendence.

Isaiah 40:21-26

Job 40:6-14

Revelation 1:12-18

God is both immanent and transcendent, but many Christians and churches in the past century have rejected the latter in order to fully embrace the former. As a result, we've fashioned a Creator in our own image who weeps, cares, and longs to help. But in the end we doubt He can actually help because we've made Him so much like ourselves. In making God our buddy, we find Him nice for cuddling but not much help when the hurricane comes.

Does your intellectual understanding of God lean more toward His immanence or His transcendence?

In your relationship with God, how do you embrace His immanent qualities?

How do you embrace God's transcendent qualities?

AN ESSENTIAL COMBINATION

Let's finish today by looking at an encounter in the Bible between God and Jacob, one that illustrates both God's transcendence and His immanence.

> *Jacob was left alone. And a man wrestled with him until the breaking of the day. When the man saw that he did not prevail against Jacob, he touched his hip socket, and Jacob's hip was put out of joint as he wrestled with him. Then he said, "Let me go, for the day has broken." But Jacob said, "I will not let you go unless you bless me." And he said to him, "What is your name?" And he said, "Jacob." Then he said, "Your name shall no longer be called Jacob, but Israel, for you have striven with God and with men, and have prevailed." Then Jacob asked him, "Please tell me your name." But he said, "Why is it that you ask my name?" And there he blessed him. So Jacob called the name of the place Peniel, saying, "For I have seen God face to face, and yet my life has been delivered."*
> Genesis 32:24-30

What strikes you as most interesting from these verses? Why?

This is a crazy story, I know. Jacob was one of the founding fathers of the Israelites, a patriarch. He knew God, but he also had a lot of problems in terms of character and decision making. So the previous story was a watershed moment in his life.

Notice first that Jacob experienced God's immanence. Now only did he have a conversation with his Creator, but he also encountered God in an intimate, physical way. Even better, he received a blessing as a result.

But also notice God's transcendence in this story. God simply touched Jacob's hip, and wham! It was put out of joint. It was a supernatural wrestling move, something that couldn't be explained rationally or logically. Even more, look at Jacob's statement in verse 30: "Jacob called the name of the place Peniel, saying, 'For I have seen God face to face, and yet my life has been delivered.' " Jacob wasn't thinking much about his blessing. He'd experienced a God who was far above his understanding, and he was grateful simply to be alive!

Let me ask you an honest question. When was the last time God took you to the mat and pinned you with a fresh awareness of His size compared to yours? You already have an idea of God's immanence, I'm sure, but when was the last time you were astonished by His transcendence? His power? His glory?

What's your answer to those questions?

Hear me on this. You must encounter God's transcendence *in addition to* His immanence if you want to truly know Him. You must train yourself to seek divine encounters and recognize when you brush against eternity. That's what we'll be exploring together in tomorrow's session.

RECOGNIZING TRANSCENDENCE

TODAY'S SCRIPTURE FOCUS   >

"Lord, you have been our dwelling place

in all generations.

Before the mountains were brought forth,

or ever you had formed the earth and the world,

from everlasting to everlasting you are God.

You return man to dust

and say, 'Return, O children of man!'

For a thousand years in your sight

are but as yesterday when it is past,

or as a watch in the night." Psalm 90:1-4

All week we've been exploring this idea of transcendence—that there's a universal longing within the human race for vertical encounters with God. But maybe you're wondering, *How do I know when I've experienced transcendence? How do I recognize a vertical encounter with God?* We're going to answer those questions today.

WHEN WE RECOGNIZE OUR SMALLNESS

First, we know we've experienced transcendence when God reminds us how small we really are. Of course, we can feel small in different ways.

A few years ago I had the privilege of visiting the White House. I was with a group of pastors who were invited from time to time to meet with the President to be briefed about different policy discussions that connected with religious life. My wife and I weren't American citizens at the time—I was born in

Canada—and so the whole thing was always a little nerve-wracking for me. I felt honored to be invited, but I was always a little nervous during the trip.

It so happened that one of these briefings took place on my birthday. I remember sitting in a richly furnished room inside the White House, looking at the big presidential seal on the podium, when somebody came out and said, "I understand one of the pastors here today is having a birthday—James MacDonald. Let's all sing 'Happy Birthday.' " So the whole group sang "Happy Birthday" to me in the White House, and I shrank down in my seat from embarrassment.

But that wasn't the worst of it. As soon as they'd finished singing, another pastor blurted out to the whole room, "He's Canadian!" I felt about two inches tall. It was humiliating.

Identify a time when you felt humiliated or ashamed.

What circumstances or factors most often make you feel humiliated? Why?

That's *not* the kind of smallness I'm talking about in experiencing transcendence. When we have a legitimate encounter with God, we don't feel humiliated or embarrassed in a negative way. Rather, we feel *appropriately* small because we recognize that we are tiny in comparison to God and His greatness. We feel gladly and joyfully small when we compare ourselves to our great God.

A true experience of eternity leaves people feeling, as C. S. Lewis said, "the infinite relief of having for once got rid of all the silly nonsense about your own dignity which has made you so restless and unhappy all your life."[4]

When have you felt appropriately small, as described above?

Was it a positive or negative experience? Why?

What circumstances or factors most often make you feel small in comparison to God's bigness?

Transcendence is a healthy dose of insignificance to a race whose root sin is pride; it cuts us down to our proper proportion before an awesome God. That's what the prophet Isaiah experienced when he was given an unprecedented view of God's glory:

In the year that King Uzziah died I saw the Lord sitting upon a throne, high and lifted up; and the train of his robe filled the temple. Above him stood the seraphim. Each had six wings: with two he covered his face, and with two he covered his feet, and with two he flew. And one called to another and said:

*"Holy, holy, holy is the LORD of hosts;
the whole earth is full of his glory!"*

And the foundations of the thresholds shook at the voice of him who called, and the house was filled with smoke. And I said: "Woe is me! For I am lost; for I am a man of unclean lips, and I dwell in the midst of a people of unclean lips; for my eyes have seen the King, the LORD of hosts!" Isaiah 6:1-5

Reread Isaiah 6:1-5. Circle any words connected with God's transcendence. Underline any words connected with Isaiah's sense of smallness.

Isaiah's encounter with God left him feeling appropriately small and more than aware of his sinful state. But he wasn't allowed to wallow in shame or humiliation.

*Then one of the seraphim flew to me, having in his hand
a burning coal that he had taken with tongs from the altar.
And he touched my mouth and said: "Behold, this has touched
your lips; your guilt is taken away, and your sin atoned for."*

*And I heard the voice of the Lord saying, "Whom shall I send,
and who will go for us?" Then I said, "Here I am! Send me."* Isaiah 6:6-8

Did you see what happened? When Isaiah caught sight of God's bigness and understood the reality of his smallness, the result was a desire to serve. That's an encounter with transcendence.

WHEN WE RECOGNIZE OUR IGNORANCE

Second, we know we've experienced transcendence when all that is knowable reminds us of how little we actually know.

I have an earned doctorate, which means I've been to more school than most, and I've read a lot beyond that. But preparing for this study has reminded me of all the books I've never experienced and of everything I don't know. In seeking to make eternity understandable, I've realized again that the sum of my knowing is fractional. It's minuscule.

It's not just the fact that so many people are smarter and know more information than I. What really amazes me is how little any of us know—or how little all of us know if you put all of our knowledge together. Think about it: only a tiny fraction of what is knowable has been discovered through scientific inquiry. Even the most learned people must humbly confess the vastness of what we don't understand.

Take a moment to think of some questions that can't be answered by scientific inquiry. Record three.

1.

2.

3.

Our lack of knowledge even extends to the only source of absolute, sufficient truth in existence, which is the Word of God. I've given my adult life thus far to the study of the book God wrote, and yet I confess to a stronger sense than I had in seminary of how vast and deep the Scriptures are—and how little I know of what God has revealed.

How have you become more aware of your limited knowledge and God's transcendence since you've become a believer?

The more we understand who God is and the truth from His Word, the more we realize how much we don't know. During those times of transcendence, a humble awareness of my own ignorance relative to all that can be known invites me to remain in awe before the One who knows the end from the beginning and everything in between. And that's a very good thing.

In the same way, I've been reminded of God's vast, incredible knowledge. The Scriptures clearly reveal that He possesses unending knowledge and unparalleled understanding. Look at Psalm 147:4-5:

> *He determines the number of the stars;*
> *he gives to all of them their names.*
> *Great is our Lord, and abundant in power;*
> *his understanding is beyond measure.*

In addition, God's knowledge isn't limited to scientific information. He knows everything about you. He knows every personal detail about you, your character, your decisions, your past, and your future.

What's your reaction to the reality that God knows all about you? Why?

When I think of all that is knowable and how little I comprehend, I can't escape the sense that I am small and that Someone exists who is greater than myself. That's a great feeling, and it leads me toward transcendence.

WHEN WE RECOGNIZE OUR FINITENESS

Third, I experience transcendence when something infinite reminds me that I am finite. David the psalmist experienced this idea when he wrote Today's Scripture Focus.

Reread Today's Scripture Focus at the beginning of today's lesson. Underline any words that express God's timelessness.

Have you ever thought deeply about the vastness of our universe? We live in a solar system (our sun and eight planets) that has a diameter of approximately 7.5 billion miles. If you drove your space car at 65 mph around the clock, it would take you 13,172 years to get across our universe. And as large as our solar system is, it's nothing when compared to our galaxy. There are over 100 billion stars in the Milky Way galaxy alone, plus additional planets revolving around their own suns. Most incredible of all, astronomers guess that there are more than 50 billion galaxies in the universe.

Our universe is incredible. It's unbelievably complicated and incomprehensibly big. But what will really knock your socks off is the knowledge that our universe is created. It was put together by Someone even bigger—Someone who is infinite.

How does an understanding of God's transcendence change your view of God?

These experiences diminish any sense of personal sovereignty, forcing me to resign again as chairman of the board of my life. Transcendence helps me accept that One exists outside the boundaries of human knowing who calls me to bow before Him and serve Him as the true center of the universe. You and I can't figure God out, but He placed inside each of us a hunger for Him. His transcendence invites us to take the focus off ourselves and seek to know the only source of true satisfaction.

Praise God for His greatness, His wisdom, and His infiniteness. Confess any pride or a horizontal focus that has kept you from recognizing God's transcendence.

1. *Oxford English Dictionary*, 3rd ed., s.v. "Transcendence."

2. Wayne Grudem, *Systematic Theology* (Downers Grove, IL: InterVarsity, 1994), 267. Available from the Internet: *http://books.google.com*.

3. A. W. Tozer, *The Knowledge of the Holy* (New York: HarperCollins, 1961), 70. Available from the Internet: *http://books.google.com*.

4. C. S. Lewis, *Mere Christianity* (New York: HarpersCollins, 1952) 127. Available from the Internet: *http://books.google.com*.

A
SINGULAR
PROVISION

GLORY

WEEK TWO

START

Welcome back to this small-group discussion of *Vertical Church*.

The application challenge from the previous session involved recording moments when you experienced the bigness and transcendence of God. If you're comfortable, describe some of those moments.

As a group, identify some common themes evident in the experiences that were discussed.

As followers of Jesus, what are some good things that can obstruct our opportunities to find fulfillment in God alone?

How has the rationalism of today's culture influenced your relationship with God?

To prepare to view the DVD segment, read these verses aloud.

> *The Lord descended in the cloud and stood with him there, and proclaimed the name of the Lord. The Lord passed before him and proclaimed, "The Lord, the Lord, a God merciful and gracious, slow to anger, and abounding in steadfast love and faithfulness, keeping steadfast love for thousands, forgiving iniquity and transgression and sin, but who will by no means clear the guilty, visiting the iniquity of the fathers on the children and the children's children, to the third and the fourth generation." And Moses quickly bowed his head toward the earth and worshiped.*
> Exodus 34:5-8

WATCH

Complete the viewer guide below as you watch DVD session 2.

The longing for _____ is satisfied only in _____.

God made you so you're _____ until you find your fulfillment in Him.

What distinguishes a person is if _____ is with them.

What makes a church distinct—powerful—is God's _____ in that church, God Himself working and manifesting Himself in spite of the weaknesses and limitations of the people involved.

Glory is the _____ of God's _____.

Blessing is what you _____. Favor is what you _____. Presence is _____ you have it. Glory is what it _____.

The universal longing is for _____.

Anytime you see God's fingerprint, that's _____.

Anytime you see glory, it shouts the existence of _____.

Glory is _____ and God's _____.

All human glory is an _____.

You were created to delight in the _____ of the One who made you. That's what fills the longing in the human heart.

No glory belongs to the created _____. All the glory belongs to the _____.

Glory is the _____ of God's _____.

There is a God. It's true in the _____ universe. It's true in the _____ universe.

VIDEO SESSIONS AVAILABLE FOR PURCHASE AT **WWW.LIFEWAY.COM/VERTICALCHURCH**

RESPOND

Discuss the DVD segment with your group, using the questions below.

> What was most interesting about the DVD segment? Why?

> Describe evidence confirming that God has been with you in recent years.

> How do you react to this statement? "What makes a church distinct—powerful—is God's presence in that church, God Himself working and manifesting Himself in spite of the weaknesses and limitations of the people involved."

> How do you define the word *glory*?

> How is God's glory connected with His transcendence? What's the difference between those two terms?

> What evidence do you see in our culture of human beings attempting to usurp God's glory?

> When have you attempted, knowingly or unknowingly, to steal the glory that belongs only to God?

APPLICATION

Spend time praising and glorifying God every day this week. Praise Him for who He is, what He's done in the world, and what He's accomplished in your life.

SCRIPTURE MEMORY FOR THIS WEEK

*How shall it be known that I have found favor in your sight,
I and your people? Is it not in your going with us, so that we are distinct,
I and your people, from every other people on the face of the earth?*
Exodus 33:16

READ WEEK 2 AND COMPLETE THE ACTIVITIES BEFORE THE NEXT GROUP EXPERIENCE.

WEEK 2

MEMORY VERSE   >

"How shall it be known that I have found favor in your sight, I and your people? Is it not in your going with us, so that we are distinct, I and your people, from every other people on the face of the earth?"

Exodus 33:16

SAY IT IN A SENTENCE   >

What God gives to satisfy the universal human longing is His glory.

BEST OF ALL   >

I've always loved the passion of pastor and revivalist John Wesley (1703–91). I'm humbled by the care he took to confirm his own salvation, his tireless work for the gospel, and his faithful endurance through nearly 90 years on earth.

Historians estimate that Wesley traveled 250,000 miles on horseback and preached more than 40,000 sermons. God used him to bring revival to two continents. As he lay on his deathbed, he gathered his family around him and summoned the strength to speak his last words. Here was a man who knew the Scriptures almost by heart and could have voiced a thousand truths in that triumphant moment.

Wesley sat up in his last 60 seconds and said, "Best of all, God is with us." Then he lay back and, thrusting his hand in the air, used his final gasp to repeat those words with emphasis: "The best of all, God is with us."

As we'll see throughout our study this week, Wesley was on to something Moses knew in the depth of his being as he struggled to lead the Israelites from Egypt to the promised land: his only point of identity, his people's only scintilla of significance, was the distinction of God's manifest presence in their midst.

The same is true for those of us who make up the church today. What separates us from all other people on the planet is the fact that God is present with us—that His glory is evident among us. What God gave to Israel in Moses' day and what He wants to give us today for our birthright as His children is the distinction of His manifest presence in our midst.

Have you experienced God's glory?

Day 1 /

EXPERIENCING GOD'S PRESENCE

TODAY'S SCRIPTURE FOCUS   >

"Jesus came and said to them, 'All authority in heaven and on earth has been given to me. Go therefore and make disciples of all nations, baptizing them in the name of the Father and of the Son and of the Holy Spirit, teaching them to observe all that I have commanded you. And behold, I am with you always, to the end of the age.' " Matthew 28:18-20

Do you like vocabulary words? I know many people who don't. They prefer to speak plainly and clearly, and they often get annoyed when others use 10-cent words in an attempt to show off. But many people genuinely love words. They're the kind of folk who buy word-of-the-day calendars every year and drop terms like *plethora* and *salacious* into everyday conversation.

If you grew up in a church and especially if you attended Sunday School, chances are good that you're familiar with three larger-than-life vocabulary words that are often used to describe God: *omnipotent*, *omniscient*, and *omnipresent*. The fact that God is omnipotent means He is all-powerful, and the fact that He's omniscient means He's all-knowing.

But it's the third word, *omnipresent*, that I want to focus on today.

UNDERSTANDING OMNIPRESENCE

Here's a quick review of this important doctrine. God is infinite, transcending all spatial limitations. His whole being fills every part of the universe. He isn't diffused anywhere but is present everywhere in all His fullness. This means the universe can't contain God. He's bigger than all creation, and He's present throughout all creation.

That's something Solomon affirmed as he supervised the construction of the temple, sometimes referred to as God's house: "Will God indeed dwell on the earth? Behold, heaven and the highest heaven cannot contain you; how much less this house that I have built!" (1 Kings 8:27).

Solomon had undoubtedly learned about God's omnipresence from his father, David, who had written these words:

> *Where shall I go from your Spirit?*
> *Or where shall I flee from your presence?*
> *If I ascend to heaven, you are there!*
> *If I make my bed in Sheol, you are there!*
> *If I take the wings of the morning*
> *and dwell in the uttermost parts of the sea,*
> *even there your hand shall lead me,*
> *and your right hand shall hold me.* Psalm 139:7-10

Record a definition of *omnipresence* in your own words.

In practical terms, what does God's omnipresence mean for His followers on earth?

Read the following passages of Scripture and record ways they contribute to your understanding of God's omnipresence.

Isaiah 66:1-2

Jeremiah 23:23-24

Colossians 1:15-17

So God is present in all places, but we need to be careful that we don't think of Him as filling up space like water in a jug. That's because "God is spirit" (John 4:24). He has no physical or material dimensions, which is good news for us. If God had mass, weight, and volume, His presence would squeeze everything else into oblivion.

Another thing we need to understand about God's omnipresence is that He doesn't behave the same way in each element of creation. I like the way Wayne Grudem, my friend and seminary professor, expressed that idea: "God does not have size or spatial dimensions and is present at every point of space with his whole being, *yet God acts differently in different places*" (emphasis added).[1]

For example, God created hell for the Devil and his minions. And though we understand that hell is defined in part by the absence of God, He could, if He desired, manifest Himself fully in hell rather than only in judgment.

Further, when Christ taught us to address God as "our Father in heaven" (Matt. 6:9), He revealed that His Father's most special and glorious self-manifestations are in the throne room of heaven. When we pray, "Your kingdom come, your will be done, on earth as it is in heaven" (v. 10), we're expressing more than an eschatological wish. We're asking God to do immediately in space and time what He does continuously in heaven and will someday do on earth in totality.

Until that day we advance God's kingdom by petitioning Him to manifest His presence in our lives and in our churches—in the precise location we're praying from in a given moment. And that's different from His omnipresence.

What's your reaction to these different aspects of God's presence? Why?

What can we learn about God from the different ways He makes Himself present in the universe and in our lives?

UNDERSTANDING MANIFEST PRESENCE

Last week we explored the longing for transcendence that's built into every human being on the planet. *Transcendence* is the best word I can think of to describe the infinite awesomeness of who God is and what He does throughout the universe, and it's something we all desperately need to experience. In fact, it's our greatest need as human beings—to experience God in a personal, life-altering way.

Here's the tricky part. When we say God is *omnipresent*, we proclaim Him to be present in all things, as we just explored. But when we use the term *transcendence,* we acknowledge God to be wholly other and entirely beyond our reach as humans.

Do you see the problem? How can God be everywhere yet also beyond our reach? This question is especially important because of the message of the gospel: that God is "actually not far from each one of us" (Acts 17:27).

How would you answer the previous question?

God manifests Himself in specific ways and at specific times to satisfy our longing for transcendence. Sometimes God draws near in a way that allows us to feel His presence and recognize His glory. I refer to this reality as God's manifest presence. And the more we experience it, the more our hunger for transcendence is satisfied.

God's manifest presence is His active engagement in the world. It refers to times when He moves beyond omnipresence and becomes directly involved in time and space. If you want to define it in a text or a tweet, manifest presence means "God @ work right here, right now!"

In other words, although God is present everywhere in the universe, upholding and sustaining His creation, He is working actively only where He wills—only where He chooses to manifest His presence.

How would you define God's manifest presence in your own words?

What are the primary ways God has made Himself known to you? In other words, when and how have you experienced His manifest presence?

In what ways have you experienced God's manifest presence in your church?

God's manifest presence is vital to our work and ministry as followers of God. And when I say vital, I don't mean it's important; I mean it's absolutely necessary for us to experience the manifest presence of God if we are to see His glory and accomplish anything for His kingdom. Just as we all long for transcendence, we all need to experience God's manifest presence in order to see His glory come down into our circumstances, our homes, our churches, and our world.

Today's Scripture Focus shows us that Jesus promised His presence at the same time He commissioned the first workers in His kingdom:

> *Jesus came and said to them, "All authority in heaven and on earth*
> *has been given to me. Go therefore and make disciples of all nations,*
> *baptizing them in the name of the Father and of the Son and of the Holy Spirit,*
> *teaching them to observe all that I have commanded you. And behold,*
> *I am with you always, to the end of the age."* Matthew 28:18-20

What emotions do you experience when you read about the work Jesus commissioned us to do? Why?

What emotions do you experience when you read Jesus' promise to be with us as we carry out that work?

Here's something else to keep in mind: God's manifest presence is never a humdrum experience. It's never boring, commonplace, or routine. It's God showing up in the world!

My friend Don Cousins, a founder of Willow Creek Community Church, has spent the past 15 years dealing with this reality as he pursues a greater experience of the supernatural in his personal life, in his family, and in the churches he serves. In his book *Unexplainable* Don wrote, "[God] wants to do the inconceivable, the uncommon, the unexpected, the remarkable, the incomprehensible, so that He—God—is the only explanation for what occurs in our lives."[2]

I couldn't agree more. And when that happens, it's because of God's manifest presence.

Which adjectives in the previous quotation describe a recent encounter you had with God? Describe what happened during that encounter.

What obstacles are blocking you from experiencing more encounters with God's manifest presence?

What steps can you take to remove those obstacles?

Day 2 /

OUR ONLY HOPE

TODAY'S SCRIPTURE FOCUS   >

"How shall it be known that I have found favor in your sight, I and your people? Is it not in your going with us, so that we are distinct, I and your people, from every other people on the face of the earth?" Exodus 33:16

As a parent, I always tried to avoid using clichés and old sayings when I spoke to my children. I never told my kids they should be seen and not heard, for example. And I avoided making the false claim that names would never hurt them.

But there's one adage I think carries some truth with it: "You never truly know what something's worth until it's gone." Or if you want the really old version, "You never miss the water until the well runs dry." I've experienced that mostly in terms of people and relationships.

Unfortunately, I think many Christians and churches today are experiencing the truth of that saying when it comes to God's manifest presence in their work and ministry. And the truly sad thing is that many of them don't even realize God's presence has moved on.

That's why we need to look at Moses today. Because if anyone understood the true value of God's presence—and terror at the thought of God's manifest presence being taken away—it was he.

MOSES WAS THE MAN

When I hear the name Moses, I picture a true colossus of a man. I see a giant in faith with a long gray beard and weary eyes. He's standing on a mountain with arms outstretched, viewing the promised land and waiting for God to take him to heaven.

I appreciate that vision of Moses, but I resonate more deeply with the Moses of early Exodus. Reared as an adopted prince of Egypt, he gradually became aware that God's preservation of his life probably carried with it certain responsibilities toward His people who were then in slavery. But the young Moses was rash and aggressive, and he tried to accomplish his calling through his own wisdom and abilities. That attempt quickly ended with a corpse buried in the sand and the pyramids in his rearview mirror.

Forty years later God gave Moses a second chance. He did it through an extraordinary combination of His transcendence and manifest presence: a bush that had caught on fire but wasn't consumed. Unfortunately, Moses was stuck on the lesson he'd learned back in Egypt: "I can't."

Read Exodus 3:1-10. What's your overall reaction to these verses? Why?

How did the burning bush reflect God's transcendence? His manifest presence?

Moses attempted to reject God's call for four different reasons. List them below in your own words and summarize how God answered each one.

Exodus 3:11

Exodus 3:13

Exodus 4:1

Exodus 4:10

I understand Moses' initial refusal to do a big job. He'd been burned by his failure in Egypt, and he'd been wallowing in the consequences of that failure for 40 years. But as with all of us, God pressed in closer and overcame his resistance by offering provision for his weakness.

Specifically, God promised Moses three things in response to his insecurities.
1. God promised miraculous signs to convince the Israelites.
2. God promised that Moses' brother Aaron would speak for him.
3. Most important of all, God promised Himself—the great I AM:

> He said, "But I will be with you, and this shall be the sign for you, that I have sent you: when you have brought the people out of Egypt, you shall serve God on this mountain." Then Moses said to God, "If I come to the people of Israel and say to them, 'The God of your fathers has sent me to you,' and they ask me, 'What is his name?' what shall I say to them?" God said to Moses, "I AM WHO I AM." And he said, "Say this to the people of Israel, 'I AM has sent me to you.' "
> Exodus 3:12-14

In the end God's greatest provision for Moses' sense of inadequacy was simply and profoundly His presence. The answer to Moses' persistent pattern of "I can't" wasn't "Yes, you can, Moses." It wasn't a bunch of rah-rah words designed to bolster Moses' self-esteem. Rather, God's provision was simply "I can; I will; I AM."

Today I'm so thankful that God offers the same provision for my inadequacies—and for yours.

When has God's presence enabled you to accomplish something beyond your own ability? What emotions and benefits resulted?

How have you seen God's manifest presence make a difference in the life and ministry of your church?

What's the difference between living self-confidently and living God-confidently?

Many amazing events took place in the days and weeks following Moses' encounter with God through a burning bush. He returned to Egypt, of course, and confronted Pharaoh with the help of his brother. Through God's provision the Israelites witnessed the plagues. They survived the Passover, were freed from their slavery, and experienced God's miraculous salvation through the parting of the Red Sea.

A TERRIFYING REALITY

Unfortunately, the reality of God's power, faithfulness, and presence didn't prevent the Israelites from experiencing spiritual distraction. The events described in Exodus 32–33 represent a shameful period in the lives of people who had just been freed from generations of slavery by God's marvelous works.

Read Exodus 32:1-14. What's the primary message of these verses?

What were the causes of the Israelites' idolatry?

The Israelites' readiness to seek alternative gods and worship idols even after witnessing so much of God's glory is frightening. It's a persistent, sobering warning to us as individuals—and to the church.

But God's response to their idolatry is truly terrifying. I'm not talking about how the Levites killed three thousand of their brothers and sisters in obedience to God's wrath. I'm not even talking about the plague that God visited on the survivors because of their idolatry, although that wasn't a happy scene. No, what's horrifying is God's declaration to Moses in chapter 33:

*The Lord said to Moses, "Depart; go up from here, you and the people
whom you have brought up out of the land of Egypt, to the land of which
I swore to Abraham, Isaac, and Jacob, saying, 'To your offspring I will give it.'
I will send an angel before you, and I will drive out the Canaanites, the Amorites,
the Hittites, the Perizzites, the Hivites, and the Jebusites. Go up to a land
flowing with milk and honey; but I will not go up among you, lest I consume
you on the way, for you are a stiff-necked people."* Exodus 33:1-3

"I will not go up among you" (v. 3). Those words sunk into Moses' heart like stones. The same was true for the rest of the Israelites, even those who had been happily worshiping an idol only a short time before. The idea of moving on without God's presence withered the spirit of everyone who heard it.

Read Exodus 33:4-16. Given the events in chapter 32, does it surprise you that the people were so devastated by God's threatened departure? Why or why not?

What does it mean that the Israelites were "stiff-necked" (v. 3)? In what ways are you stiff-necked as well?

Look at verses 12-16. How would you describe Moses' emotions during this conversation?

Even though God committed to continue His manifest presence with the children of Israel (see v. 14), Moses didn't hear it. He kept right on stating his case. That's kind of funny, but notice the reason Moses missed God's response. He was so furious at the situation—at the unutterable nightmare of taking even a single step without God's manifest presence—that he couldn't stop freaking out.

When I read that, I ask myself, *Am I that terrified to walk a mile in ministry without the manifest presence of God? Does the thought of a weekend service, a counseling appointment, or a meeting with church leaders—apart from God's abiding presence—put me in meltdown mode?*

It should, and Moses did a great job of expressing the reason: "Is it not in your going with us, so that we are distinct, I and your people, from every other people on the face of the earth?" (v. 16).

As with the children of Israel, God's presence is the vertical connection that makes Christians distinct from the world around us. His presence is the one thing that gives us access to His glory.

How is God's presence evident in your life? In your church?

What challenge are you facing that you know you can't overcome on your own? How will you seek God's presence and invite Him into your circumstance?

SEEING HIS GLORY

TODAY'S SCRIPTURE FOCUS   >

"The LORD said to Moses, 'This very thing that you have spoken I will do, for you have found favor in my sight, and I know you by name.' Moses said, 'Please show me your glory.' " Exodus 33:17-18

The Bible is filled with the stories of many great men and women, but I don't think anyone had a more outstanding life—a more eye-opening, ground-shaking experience on this planet—than Moses.

I commend Moses' life so much because he had a relationship with the Lord unlike any other human who's ever lived. Sure, Elijah and Enoch didn't die, but Moses talked with God face-to-face, "as a man speaks to his friend" (Ex. 33:11). Joseph was awesome in leading his family down to Egypt and administrating the nation during a famine under its pharaoh. But Moses brought a pharaoh to his knees and led a whole nation of slaves out of bondage under the banner of 10 miraculous signs, by way of a God-opened sea. Ezekiel was as faithful as a prophet could be in delivering the message of God in difficult circumstances, but Moses led millions to a mountain where he got Ten Commandments engraved by the finger of God.

Bottom line: Moses had a front-row seat to God's grand, spectacular work like no other person in history. So we should pay attention to Moses' bold, audacious request in Today's Scripture Focus.

SHOW ME YOUR GLORY

Remember, the majority of Exodus 33 describes a horrible situation for Moses and the Israelites. God told Moses His presence would no longer accompany His people as they journeyed to the promised land, and Moses—terrified and furious at the same time—begged God to change His mind.

Then came this startling exchange:

> *The LORD said to Moses, "This very thing that you have spoken*
> *I will do, for you have found favor in my sight, and I know you*
> *by name." Moses said, "Please show me your glory."* Exodus 33:17-18

Why do you think God said He was pleased with Moses?

Why do you think Moses requested to see God's glory?

Don't miss the first part of those verses. Can you imagine what it would be like to hear God say you've found favor in His sight? That He knows your name? I know people who get excited when they shake hands with a celebrity or receive an autograph. But can you imagine what it would be like to have the Creator of the universe say, "I know who you are. I know your name. And I'm pleased with you"?

The only thing more incredible is that we all have the same opportunity. That's what C. S. Lewis wrote about in *The Weight of Glory:*

> *I read in a periodical the other day that the fundamental thing is how
> we think of God. By God Himself, it is not! How God thinks of us is not only
> more important, but infinitely more important . ... It is written that we shall
> "stand before" Him, shall appear, shall be inspected. The promise of glory
> is the promise, almost incredible and only possible by the work of Christ,
> that some of us, that any of us who really chooses, shall actually survive that
> examination, shall find approval, shall please God. To please God—to be a real
> ingredient in the divine happiness—to be loved by God, not merely pitied, but
> delighted in as an artist delights in his work or a father in a son—it seems impossible,
> a weight or burden of glory which our thoughts can hardly sustain. But so it is.[3]*

Read 2 Corinthians 5:6-10. What emotions do you experience when reading these verses? Why?

Do you believe God is pleased with you? Why or why not?

Read Matthew 25:14-30. What emotions do you experience when reading these verses? Why?

Let's get back to Moses. Sensing God's tender heart for his weariness and frustration with the stubborn people he was called to lead, Moses went for the brass ring: "Please show me your glory" (Ex. 33:18).

Read Exodus 33:19-23. What were the restrictions God placed on Moses' seeing His glory?

Why were those restrictions necessary?

Read Exodus 34:29-35. What was the result of Moses' experiences with God?

The glory of God the Father is the glory that Moses saw, and it's the very purpose for the existence of the universe. When transcendence comes near, we call it manifest presence, but it's really the glory of God. Let's study the word *glory* in more detail, because it must be the goal of every ministry activity in a vertical church.

DEFINING *GLORY*

The phrase "your glory" (Ex. 33:18) literally means *your weight*. It's the idea of *your significance, your scope, your capacity*. Moses asked to see the fullest expression of the only God.

What words or images come to your mind when you see the term *glory*?

Glory is used 199 times in the Old Testament. In the Greek translation of the Old Testament, the Jewish translators chose the word *doxa*, which English borrowed for the word *doxology*. *Doxa* means *the light that comes from something brilliant*. Its only proper use is in regard to God. Jonathan Edwards said glory is "[God's] infinite knowledge, His infinite … holiness, His infinite joy and happiness."[4] But Edwards was giving expressions of glory rather than a definition of what it actually is.

Glory is a manifestation of God's reality. Think of it this way. As heat is to fire, glory is to God. As wet is to water, glory is to God. As light is to the sun, glory is to God. Glory is what emanates from God.

When someone or something demonstrates the reality of God's existence, that revelation is God's glory. We don't see God; we see the evidence that He has been at work. We see His glory. That's why God answered Moses as He did: "Moses, you can't see Me. Nobody 'sees' Me and lives. If you look at the sun for five seconds, your eyes will burn out. Do you know I made more than 50 billion suns by a single word from My mouth? You don't know what you're asking, Moses. No man can see Me and live."

Read the following passages of Scripture and record what they teach you about God.

1 Timothy 6:13-16

Hebrews 12:28-29

Glory is the maximum we can handle of seeing the Lord; it's the fingerprint of God left on everything He touches in the universe and in His church. Anytime you see evidence of God, you're seeing glory. A beautiful sunset that illumines the western sky shouts the majesty of the Maker and declares His glory. A newborn baby coughs his first breath and sucks enough oxygen to scream through his little tears, "There's a God!" Learn to lean in and listen as the miracle of life manifests the glory of God:

> *The heavens declare the glory of God,*
> *and the sky above proclaims his handiwork.*
> *Day to day pours out speech,*
> *and night to night reveals knowledge.*
> *There is no speech, nor are there words,*
> *whose voice is not heard.*
> *Their voice goes out through all the earth,*
> *and their words to the end of the world.* Psalm 19:1-4

How have you seen God's glory reflected in creation?

In what ways is the fingerprint of God's glory visible in your life?

How is God's glory visible in your church?

The glory of creation is shouting, "There's a God who made it all!" The purpose of life is to discover that truth and the infinite satisfaction that can be found only by living in a community that is reveling in glory and bringing others into that experience.

That's why we're here: to discover the God who made us, to live for His glory, and to show off how awesome He is so that others can see His glory too.

GLORY IS FOR GOD ALONE

TODAY'S SCRIPTURE FOCUS >

"For my own sake, for my own sake, I do it,

for how should my name be profaned?

My glory I will not give to another.

Listen to me, O Jacob,

and Israel, whom I called!

I am he; I am the first,

and I am the last." Isaiah 48:11-12

In the summer of 1945, right at the end of the Second World War, many soldiers were returning home from combat, including many professional athletes who'd been drafted to serve. One of those returning soldiers was Joe DiMaggio.

Though he hadn't played baseball for years, DiMaggio took his four-year-old son one day and slipped into the stands where the Yankees were playing, excited just to take in a game. The fans around him were thrilled when they saw the great Joe DiMaggio sitting in the stands with his son. It started with just two or three persons, but then more and more started to chant, "Joe, Joe DiMaggio." Eventually, the whole crowd was calling out the rhyme, chanting, "Joe, Joe DiMaggio," shouting it in appreciation.

In the midst of the chant and the cheers, DiMaggio's little four-year-old, Joe Jr., looked up at his father and said, "See, Daddy? Everyone knows me."

That story is funny for a child embracing the glory that belonged to his earthly father as though he deserved it. But it's a tragic and serious tale when we as pastors, leaders, and church members embrace the glory that belongs to God alone as though we deserve it.

What does it look like when a human being attempts to accept or indulge in God's glory?

When have you made the mistake of seeking glory that rightfully belongs to God?

GOD ALONE

The idea of glory frequently comes up in connection with human beings. We refer to the glory of our countries, for example. We say that athletes or movie stars receive honor and glory when they perform at the pinnacle of their abilities.

But the reality is that true glory—the kind of glory that's reflected in the deepest recesses of the universe—belongs to God alone. He's the only One who creates and receives that kind of glory.

Read Isaiah 48:6-16. What words and phrases stand out to you in these verses? Why?

What can we learn about God from these verses?

What can we learn about God's glory?

One of our neighbors on a street where we used to live was cranky to the max if anyone came near anything that was his. If our kids, walking home from school, ever put their feet on the corner of his lawn, he ran onto his porch and screamed, "Get off my grass!" in total meltdown mode.

God isn't like that. When He says, "My glory I will not give to another" (v. 11), He's not being a grumpy, selfish deity protecting His turf because He wrongly values His glory or fears its diminishment. No, God doesn't share His glory because He won't, for our sakes, allow us to claim something that isn't true.

Remember, glory is God's fingerprint. It's the evidence of His work in the universe. Therefore, if God allowed us to take glory for ourselves, it would only promote our ignorance. It would lead us to remain confused about who God is—and who isn't God.

This picture is illustrated very effectively in the demise of a man named Herod:

> *On an appointed day Herod put on his royal robes, took his seat upon the throne, and delivered an oration to them. And the people were shouting, "The voice of a god, and not of a man!" Immediately an angel of the Lord struck him down, because he did not give God the glory, and he was eaten by worms and breathed his last. But the word of God increased and multiplied.* Acts 12:21-24

What's your reaction to those verses? Why?

Do you ever fear the consequences of attempting to usurp God's glory? Why or why not?

I love the way that passage of Scripture ends. For all of Herod's wealth, power, and gifted speech, he ended up the same way we all do—eaten by worms. And just to make sure we all understand where the glory belonged, verse 24 reminds us, "The word of God increased and multiplied."

We'll never experience the delight of God's glory if we insist on pretending it belongs to us. God is glorious, and He's given us the chance to participate in His wonderful, amazing plans for the universe. He's given us the opportunity to serve Him and others in ways that matter for eternity. But we'll receive no joy from that participation if we maintain a fantasy that we're the driving force behind everything being accomplished. We only make a mockery of our opportunities.

What do you enjoy most about serving God and others? Why?

When do you catch yourself feeling prideful in the midst of that service? In other words, what commonly triggers your pride?

Have you ever complimented someone, and then they responded by saying something like "I'm just giving the glory to God"? We can be tempted to roll our eyes at those statements, assuming they're expressions of false modesty, but we need to be careful about such thoughts. Because giving glory to God is exactly what we're supposed to do when any type of horizontal glory comes our way.

When I say we should give glory to God, I'm not talking about reluctantly sharing what we have, as if we have a basketful of glory and we're willing to pass some handfuls over to God. I'm talking about a truthful reflection of what others confuse as ours but we can't rightly accept. In other words, refusing glory isn't false humility; it's not even genuine humility. It's just honesty.

How do you respond when people praise your accomplishments in ministry?

How can we reflect glory vertically to Christ without sounding pompous or falsely humble?

Psalm 115:1 expresses this idea well:

> *Not to us, O LORD, but to your name give glory,*
> *for the sake of your steadfast love and your faithfulness!*

The psalmist voiced the surrender of a man who'd fought too long in a struggle that can't be won. He'd learned a universal lesson: to embrace the reality that our happiness isn't found in increasing our own glory but in giving ourselves to the glory of God.

OUR CONSUMING PASSION

Giving glory to God and reflecting to Him any glory that people try to send our way shouldn't be a passive activity or something of mild interest to us. It should be the consuming passion of our lives.

Remember when Moses came down from Mount Sinai and found the Israelites engaged in a full-blown worship service directed not at God but at a golden lump of metal in the shape of a cow? He wasn't miffed; he wasn't peeved. He was filled with righteous fury because of his passion for God's glory.

Look again at Exodus 32:15-29. What's your response to Moses' actions in these verses?

Look specifically at Aaron's words that begin in verse 22. What excuses did he give for the Israelites' behavior?

Notice that Moses held Aaron responsible for the desecration of God's glory. Today it's church leaders' responsibility to be jealous for the glory of God in their churches. If we don't insist on the manifest presence of God as the motivation for all we do, no one else will—least of all God.

Something inside us must revolt when we see singers seeking glory for themselves or preachers parading their personalities in a way that detracts from God's glory. In our souls we must determine to focus on what honors God and what brings Him the most glory. That's the ground we must constantly choose to defend.

Where are the danger zones in churches where individuals or whole groups of people often focus on horizontal glory rather than vertical glory?

What can be done to reestablish a vertical conduit of glory in those areas? What can you do specifically?

God's glory is the purpose of the ages—the reason everything exists and the only reason we get to draw another breath this moment. God desires that in every action we display the glorious reality of the One who made us. May it be so in your life today.

UNHINDERED GLORY

TODAY'S SCRIPTURE FOCUS   >

"Behold, the Lord's hand is not shortened, that it cannot save,

or his ear dull, that it cannot hear;

but your iniquities have made a separation

between you and your God,

and your sins have hidden his face from you

so that he does not hear." Isaiah 59:1-2

Barriers are everywhere in the world today, and sometimes that's a good thing. When you drive down an interstate, for example, you may see a concrete divider separating the two lanes of traffic. That's a good barrier. It prevents head-on collisions.

But there are a lot of bad barriers in the world as well. Guilt, shame, and a lack of self-confidence are all barriers that can keep us from achieving our dreams in life. Hatred and bigotry are barriers that prevent people from joining together in meaningful ways.

Today we'll explore what it looks like to live for the glory of God. But first we need to examine one of the primary barriers that often prevents us from experiencing God's glory and presence.

THE SIN BARRIER

We all understand that sin creates a barrier separating unbelievers from the joy of God's presence and that Jesus Christ's death on the cross opened the door for the sin barrier to be removed. That's the gospel: "All have sinned and fall short of the glory of God, and are justified by his grace as a gift, through the redemption that is in Christ Jesus, whom God put forward as a propitiation by his blood, to be received by faith" (Rom. 3:23-25).

But do you realize that sin in the believing community creates a barrier between us and God's manifest presence? The glory that leads to salvation must also play an active role in our sanctification as Christ followers. That's the message of the Scriptures.

Read Isaiah 59:1-8. Which images do you find most interesting in these verses? Why?

What specific sins did God accuse the Israelites of committing?

In a similar way, one of the psalmists wrote:

> *If I had cherished iniquity in my heart,*
> *the Lord would not have listened.*
> *But truly God has listened;*
> *he has attended to the voice of my prayer.* Psalm 66:18-19

God distances Himself from and disdains church gatherings where worship has become formulaic, where sin is unresolved, and where hearts are callous to issues of mercy and justice for the poor.

Read Isaiah 1:11-15. What was God's primary message to the people of Israel in these verses?

What specific sins did God accuse them of committing?

What are the connections between these verses and the church today?

Our actions affect God's manifest presence when our churches gather to worship. This is why Jesus instructed us to abandon our expression of worship at the altar until we've done our best to reconcile over any issue of hatred (see Matt. 5:23-24). Why leave the gift when hatred hinders worship?

Do we come to church conscious that every action and motive promotes or discourages God's manifest presence? We should, because that's exactly what happens. Every note, every spoken word, every attitude from every usher, every motive of every vocalist—all of it is seen and known by a holy God whose desire is to manifest His presence among His people and is welcomed or spurned by us.

The same is true of our personal connections with God. Our embrace of sin and rebellion pushes God away and prevents us from experiencing the reason we've been created: to live for God's glory.

How could church leaders tell whether sin in the community was creating a barrier to God's manifest presence? What symptoms would be evident in that church?

How could individuals tell whether their sin was limiting their ability to experience God's manifest presence? What symptoms would be evident in that person's life? Are you currently experiencing any such symptoms?

WHEN GOD MANIFESTS HIS PRESENCE

When we experience Gods' manifest presence in our lives and in our churches, we live in a way that reflects glory back to Him. There's no formula that can calculate or measure God's presence. There's no instrument that makes it clear whether God's glory has come down. But certain indicators reveal whether we're experiencing His glory as individuals and as the body of Christ.

For individuals, the evidence of God's manifest presence and reflected glory can largely be observed by looking for the fruit of the Spirit:

> *The works of the flesh are evident: sexual immorality, impurity, sensuality, idolatry, sorcery, enmity, strife, jealousy, fits of anger, rivalries, dissensions, divisions, envy, drunkenness, orgies, and things like these. ... But the fruit of the Spirit is love, joy, peace, patience, kindness, goodness, faithfulness, gentleness, self-control; against such things there is no law.* Galatians 5:19-23

Which of the "works of the flesh" (v. 19) are evident in your life right now? What steps can you take to remove them?

Which of the "fruit of the Spirit" (v. 22) are evident in your life right now? Which are missing? What steps can you take to increase your demonstration of this fruit?

When you look at an entire church, one way to see evidence of God's manifest presence is to look for the fruit of the Spirit in the lives of individual members. That's not easy to evaluate, so here's corporate evidence that God's glory is present in a vertical church.

1. Expectant prayer frequently occurs before, after, and during the worship service, including petitions for God's grace for healing work at every level: mind, emotions, and body.

2. Powerful, biblical preaching gives listeners a distinct sense of hearing God speak with authority to their souls in a way that brings Holy Spirit conviction they can't deny or dismiss.

3. Passionate, expressive worship—in which voices are loud, hands are raised, tears flow, minds are expanded, and hearts are moved—gives evidence that Christ is adored.

4. Individual salvation, proportionate to the size of the church, regularly and continuously occurs in large numbers because people want their friends to experience what they have.

5. Racial, economic, language, and generational diversity grows because what members have in common in the Lord is far greater than the things that separate.

6. The majority of adults gather in smaller groups to stir up, spur on, and support their walks with God. Relationships flourish and follow the biblical pattern of grace and truth.

7. Elders lead, discord isn't tolerated, and people are held to account. Leaders also listen and learn, loving people and letting the unity of the Spirit be enjoyed by all who work to keep it.

8. Christ reigns and is increasingly exalted as Head in people's hearts, so that gratitude overflows into graciousness and generosity. Christians become disciples, disciples become leaders, and leaders are frequently sent to plant churches nearby and around the globe.

9. The needs of the poor are met, prisoners are visited, aliens are welcomed as friends, strangers are served as brothers, and widows are cared for. These priorities aren't programs or phases but the lasting overflow of God's abundance in members' hearts.

10. Everyone sees, knows, feels, and delights in the evidence that theirs is a vertical church.

Which of the previous characteristics have you experienced in church? Which are you experiencing now?

Are you contributing to these evidences of God's presence in your church, or are you a barrier to His presence? Explain your answer.

What steps can you take to experience a greater measure of God's manifest presence and reflect His glory in your community?

1. Wayne Grudem, *Systematic Theology* (Downers Grove, IL: InterVarsity, 1994), 173. Available from the Internet: *http://books.google.com.*

2. Don Cousins, *Unexplainable: Pursuing a Life Only God Can Make Possible* (Colorado Springs: David C. Cook, 2009), 14–15. Available from the Internet: *http://books.google.com.*

3. C. S. Lewis, *Weight of Glory* (New York: HarperCollins, 1949), 38–39. Available from the Internet: *http://books.google.com.*

4. Jonathan Edwards, "The End for Which God Created the World," in John Piper, *God's Passion for His Glory: Living the Vision of Jonathan Edwards* (Wheaton, IL: Crossway, 2006), 244. Available from the Internet: *http://books.google.com.*

A
COMMON
ACCESS

CHURCH

WEEK THREE

START

Welcome back to this small-group discussion of *Vertical Church*.

The application challenge from the previous session involved intentionally praising and glorifying God every day. If you're comfortable, describe experiences you felt were meaningful or powerful.

What did you like best from week 2 in the workbook? What questions do you still have?

Work together as a group to come up with a definition of God's manifest presence.

How have you seen God's presence manifested in your church? In your life?

To prepare to view the DVD segment, read these verses aloud.

*"For this reason I bow my knees before the Father, from whom every family
in heaven and on earth is named, that according to the riches of his glory
he may grant you to be strengthened with power through his Spirit
in your inner being, so that Christ may dwell in your hearts through
faith—that you, being rooted and grounded in love, may have strength
to comprehend with all the saints what is the breadth and length
and height and depth, and to know the love of Christ that surpasses
knowledge, that you may be filled with all the fullness of God."*
Ephesians 3:14-19

WATCH

Complete the viewer guide below as you watch DVD session 3.

▌ **The glory of God is the _____ of the universe.**

▌ **The glory of God is _____ in Jesus Christ.**

The Word became flesh on the earth and dwelt among us and lived a perfect _____ so that He could die a substitutionary _____ and take upon Himself the wrath of Almighty God for your sin and mine.

The awesome thing is that God has made _____ for our stubborn rebellion in His Son, Jesus Christ. That's the glory.

Don't ever cease to be shocked by the wonder and amazed by the power of the message of the _____.

The awesome thing about Jesus is that He is full of _____ and full of _____—grace not diminished by truth, truth not diminished by grace.

Everything God wants you to know about Himself, God the Father, is in _____ _____.

▌ **A common access: _____**

▌ **The church is the _____ of God's _____ .**

▌ We do ministry in a way that shows off how awesome _____ is.

▌ **The church is the _____ of Christ's _____.**

▌ Christ _____ the church.

▌ **The church is the _____ of Christ's _____.**

▌ We're on a winning _____ in a winning _____.

▌ **The church is the _____ of Christ's _____.**

▌ The goal was not to save you. That was the first step in the bigger mission, which was to _____ you; it means to change you, to set you apart, to make you _____.

RESPOND

Discuss the DVD segment with your group, using the questions below.

> What did you like most about the DVD segment? Why?

> In your own words, what's the primary message of the gospel?

> Work together as a group to define the difference between grace and truth.

> In light of those definitions, what does it mean that Jesus is "full of grace and truth" (John 1:14)?

> What words and images come to mind when you hear the word *church*? Why?

> How do you react to this statement? "[The church] is the hope of the world. It's where Jesus put all of His eggs—in the church basket. He loves the church and gave Himself for it."

> How have you benefited most from the churches you've attended? What improvements would you like to see in the church as a whole?

APPLICATION

Conduct a prayer walk at your church this week during a time when the building is mostly vacant. As you walk around the grounds or through the halls, pray that God's glory would be manifest in that place for you and the other members of your community to experience in a powerful way.

SCRIPTURE MEMORY FOR THIS WEEK

The Word became flesh and dwelt among us, and we have seen his glory, glory as of the only Son from the Father, full of grace and truth.
John 1:14

READ WEEK 3 AND COMPLETE THE ACTIVITIES BEFORE THE NEXT GROUP EXPERIENCE.

WEEK 3

MEMORY VERSE >

"The Word became flesh and dwelt among us, and we have seen his glory, glory as of the only Son from the Father, full of grace and truth."

John 1:14

SAY IT IN A SENTENCE >

The glory of Jesus Christ revealed fuels the fire of a vertical church.

ONE PLACE >

Those of us living in North America today have an almost unlimited number of avenues and opportunities to get whatever we need. That's something I'm reminded of every day as I drive down Randall Road toward the main campus of our church in Elgin, Illinois.

Randall Road is a north-south corridor that stretches for more than 30 miles on the western edge of the Chicago suburbs. The highway passes through more than 10 separate townships and villages in those 30 miles, and it's packed with just about every retail store you can imagine.

For example, if I leave our Elgin campus and drive south on Randall Road for just 20 minutes, I'll pass three separate Target Superstores, plus two Meijers and two Walmarts. If I'm in the mood for an authentic Chicago-style pizza, I'm five minutes away from Giordano's. If I'm craving a real Chicago-style hot dog, I can make a beeline for Portillo's. If I need a new TV, I can head to Best Buy. If I need a new dog, I can stop at PetSmart. If I'm in the middle of a project at home and can't find an important tool, I have my choice of Home Depot, Lowe's, or Ace to grab a replacement.

You get the idea.

And yet the more I find myself surrounded by retail stores and outlet malls, the more I'm reminded of this vital truth: there's only one place on the face of the earth where I can get what I need the most, the place where God has promised to reveal the glory of His great Son, Jesus Christ, and that's the church. God's revealed glory is not promised to the health club or the school cafeteria or the mall. God never said or even hinted that He'd display His manifest presence at flea markets or political conventions or football stadiums. Glory isn't promised to parachurch organizations or even to Christian homes.

No. What we've identified as eternity/transcendence/manifest presence/glory is promised only when we gather in Jesus' name as the church.

THE RADIANCE OF GOD'S GLORY

TODAY'S SCRIPTURE FOCUS >

"Long ago, at many times and in many ways, God spoke to our fathers by the prophets, but in these last days he has spoken to us by his Son, whom he appointed the heir of all things, through whom also he created the world. He is the radiance of the glory of God and the exact imprint of his nature, and he upholds the universe by the word of his power. After making purification for sins, he sat down at the right hand of the Majesty on high."

Hebrews 1:1-3

Are you ready for a little review? We're already in week 3 of this study, so let's take a moment to look back and see what we've covered.

We learned in week 1 that God has placed a universal longing for transcendence in every human heart. We saw in week 2 that God's glory eclipses all other transcendent experiences in the universe. Our job as disciples is to unveil our great God and trust Him to shine and show who He is in the hearts He's drawing to Himself.

This week we're going to talk about the church, which is our common access to God's glory, but I want to start by focusing on Jesus over the next couple days. That's because Jesus is the foundation of the church. It's His body, and He's the Head. Without His actions on our behalf, there'd be no church at all! We'll finish the week by exploring why the church is God's designated place for unveiling His glory.

GOD'S GLORY REVEALED IN JESUS

Eternity. Transcendence. Glory. Manifest presence. Those are all important concepts, I would say vital concepts, but none of them are particularly concrete. None of them are easily communicated. So here's an important question: what specifically do we as the church have to offer people that reveals who God is and what we need from Him?

We find the answer to those questions in Today's Scripture Focus.

Read Today's Scripture Focus at the beginning of this lesson. What can we learn about Jesus from these verses?

Why is Jesus a better spokesperson for God's glory than the Old Testament prophets?

The glory of God is revealed in Jesus Christ. The glory our hearts were created to long for—the glory whispered by the universe all around us—God has shouted to us in the form of His Son, Jesus Christ. And that's what we as members of the church, the body of Christ, are called to unveil to the world. That's the best thing we can offer to explain what God is like.

This point is so central to the New Testament that if you miss it, you'll miss everything. So let's spend some time exploring a Scripture where this message of glory is concentrated: the Gospel of John. In fact, sometimes it seems as if the apostle John could hardly write a paragraph describing what he'd seen and heard without encapsulating it all in the word *glory*—starting in chapter 1.

Read John 1:1-14. What words and phrases stand out to you most in these verses? Why?

What can we learn about Jesus from these verses? Make a list of at least five things.

1.

2.

3.

4.

5.

This is the kind of passage we need to read out loud to fully appreciate. The energy and focus of John's words swell and build until we reach that monumental declaration in verse 14: "The Word became flesh and dwelt among us." Gasp! Our creative God—this Light and Life of men and women, this Word—chose to become manifest in the world, incarnated as flesh, and live among us.

What emotions do you experience when you contemplate the gospel story? Why?

How does the gospel reveal God's glory?

How does your life reflect God's glory that's revealed in Jesus Christ?

Look again at John 1:14. What word did John use to narrow the focus of the passage? It isn't *love*, *wisdom*, or *perfection*, although all those were visible in Jesus' life. It's *glory!* We've seen His glory.

The glory of God is revealed in Jesus Christ. Don't ever get tired of this story. God can't reveal Himself in any greater way than what He's done in Jesus Christ.

GRACE AND TRUTH

While we're focused on John 1:14, I want to point out something interesting about the end of the verse. The glory of Jesus includes the fact that He's "full of grace and truth." He's bursting with grace, acceptance, and love for those who need it, and that's wonderful. But He's no less full of truth about our sinfulness and its consequences, and that's just as wonderful.

Look at the following passages of Scripture and record whether they illustrate Jesus' grace, truth, or both.

Matthew 8:5-13

Matthew 10:34-39

Luke 10:38-42

John 4:1-30

Unlike Jesus, we tend to be either grace people or truth people by nature, and we usually align ourselves with one and neglect the other, so we're greatly in need of the balance Jesus brings.

What can happen when believers focus too much on truth?

What can happen when believers focus too much on grace?

Truth-focused people stand strong, hold the line, and demand conformity to the letter of the law, but they can end up being judgmental and legalistic. There's no glory in that. At the same time, grace-focused people delight in the God of second chances, but they can quickly slip into a superficial, smiley world where you can't say "sin" and you emphasize love without the demands of biblical truth. There's no glory in that either. Until people see more of both grace and truth in us, we won't make progress toward becoming like Christ.

Are you more of a truth person or a grace person? Explain your answer.

What has occurred in your life or in your spiritual growth that has shown you the need to be more balanced in expressing truth and grace?

I began life as a truth guy, and my failings at following Jesus' balanced example are legion when it comes to being full of grace. Fortunately, while I pray that truth is never diminished in my preaching or disciple making, God has graciously pursued me through much pain about the need to "be strong in … grace" (2 Tim. 2:1, NKJV).

Why does this matter? Because when we represent only one half of Jesus' character, we put a shade in front of His glory reflected in our lives. We create shadows in places that are supposed to burst with the light of Christ.

When I look back, it's clear that when I've failed in offering grace, I've restricted God's glory in my life and ministry, and often our church has suffered for my deficiencies. Yet where my grace has grown to be more in line with Christ's exemplary fullness, our ministry has reached new levels of revealed glory.

I pray the same will be true in your life as you reflect God's transcendent glory revealed in Jesus Christ.

Identify any areas of your life in which are you restricting God's reflected glory by neglecting grace or truth. What can you do to express grace and truth in a more balanced way this week?

EXPERIENCING GLORY

TODAY'S SCRIPTURE FOCUS   >

"I do not ask for these only, but also for those who will believe in me through their word, that they may all be one, just as you, Father, are in me, and I in you, that they also may be in us, so that the world may believe that you have sent me. The glory that you have given me I have given to them, that they may be one even as we are one, I in them and you in me, that they may become perfectly one, so that the world may know that you sent me and loved them even as you loved me." John 17:20-23

Biblical literacy is on the decline in modern society. Many people have almost no clue about the different people and events recorded in the Bible, let alone the life lessons and spiritual guidelines that can be gleaned from those people and events. Sadly, this deterioration is affecting members of the church as well as the general population.

But there's one area of the Bible that continues to penetrate our various cultural lexicons, and that's the miracles of Jesus. Those events stood out during His life on earth, and they continue to stand out today. For example, if I say, "That person's great, but he doesn't walk on water," most people know whom I'm referring to.

What are your favorite miracles from Jesus' life and ministry? Record your top three and note the reasons they resonate with you.

1.

2.

3.

THE *WHY* OF JESUS' MIRACLES

Have you ever wondered why Jesus performed His miracles? Sure, they were flashy, and they obviously made an impression on people. But what was the underlying purpose of those supernatural acts? We get an answer in John 2, when Jesus performed His first miracle: turning water into wine during the wedding feast in Cana.

Read John 2:1-11. What do you find most interesting about these verses? Why?

What was the result of this miracle? What happened in the lives of people who witnessed it?

This is a well-known story even in today's culture, but what's not well understood is verse 11: "This, the first of his signs, Jesus did at Cana in Galilee, and manifested his glory. And his disciples believed in him." Notice this was just the first of Jesus' signs; it was only the beginning. Where Jesus is at work, things happen that can't be explained by human reason.

Also notice the two words John used to describe the purpose behind Jesus' miracles: *manifest* and *glory*. We've seen those words more than a few times throughout this study, right? Glory is what God gives to satisfy the longing He placed in every human heart, and John says Jesus' miracles were one way He manifested that glory in a way that people could observe and experience. And it worked. John said, "His disciples believed in him."

We see something similar in Jesus' last recorded miracle in the Gospel of John, when He raised Lazarus from the dead. You know that story. Mary and Martha were Jesus' dear friends, so the disciples expected Jesus to hurry to their side when they sent word that their brother, Lazarus, was dying. But Jesus stayed put. He delayed for two whole days. And then He said something incredible: "This illness does not lead to death. It is for the glory of God, so that the Son of God may be glorified through it" (John 11:4).

When Jesus finally arrived on the scene—after Lazarus had died—Jesus reminded Mary and Martha that anything, even the darkest moments of our suffering, can reveal His glory: "Did I not tell you that if you believed you would see the glory of God?" (v. 40).

Hear this: when Christians are taught that their ultimate purpose is reaching the lost or building a church or extending their hand to the poor, their commitment to Christ usually derails during difficult times. That's because horizontal purposes, even ones that express God's heart for the lost and hurting, are not adequate to sustain a lifetime of devotion to the gospel through the valleys people invariably face. Believers without a clear vertical connection with God will not survive hard times if the focus of their lives is horizontal obedience. We need to understand that.

We also need to understand that this glory—this manifest presence of God—is the only "product" the church has to offer. When every pastor in North America gets hold of the reality that we are providers of nothing but we are merely facilitators of God's glory, then and only then will churches return to their created purpose. Even more, when every member of the church realizes that we are all just individual channels through whom Christ can reveal Himself, we'll see God begin to move in power and display His glory in ways that change lives.

Think of a time when you've suffered greatly (maybe that's right now). How was Jesus' glory reflected in your suffering? How could it have been reflected more?

What does it mean to be a facilitator of God's glory?

Think of a time when you've seen God do something powerful in your life, family, or church. What led up to God's actions? What were the results?

THE TWO-WAY STREET

Let's review three points about God's glory.
1. Jesus is the radiance of God's glory. He's the full and perfect expression of God's glory, yet He took the incomprehensible step of incarnating Himself down in the dirt with us.
2. Jesus and His glory are the foundation of the church.
3. Those of us who make up the church are facilitators of Jesus' glory; we are a collection of conduits through which Jesus can reveal Himself.

The next thing we need to understand is that God's glory runs vertically, not horizontally. It runs up and down, not side to side.

The first part of this two-way street is that we are called to glorify God. Several passages of Scripture testify to our responsibility in this area, including Romans 15:5-6:

> *May the God of endurance and encouragement grant you to live in such harmony with one another, in accord with Christ Jesus, that together you may with one voice glorify the God and Father of our Lord Jesus Christ.*

Read the following passages of Scripture and record ways they instruct us to glorify God.

Matthew 5:14-16

1 Corinthians 6:12-20

2 Corinthians 12:7-10

Let me be clear about one thing: God doesn't need our glory. He gets no benefit from our efforts to glorify Him, just as a mountain receives no benefits from a pile of dirt or an ocean receives no glory from birdbaths. Jesus Christ doesn't receive glory from people.

Rather, it's for *our* benefit that we give glory to God. When we send up our shouts of glory to God, He responds with a roar of glory that pours down in a river throughout the church. That's the second part of the two-way street. We look up to glorify God, and He sends a flood of glory back down to us. It's vertical, and it flows both ways.

But everything gets messed up when we start glorifying things on a horizontal level. That's what Jesus made clear in John 5.

Read John 5:30-47. What words or phrases catch your attention in these verses? Why?

What do these verses communicate about worship on a horizontal level?

Verse 44 is the key: "How can you believe, when you receive glory from one another and do not seek the glory that comes from the only God?" Recently I was so arrested by that verse in my quiet time that I posted it on the bulletin board behind my computer. I've always understood that taking glory belonging to God is sinful. We're supposed to deflect any glory pointed at us so that we can reflect the glory of Jesus.

What I didn't understand is that accepting glory on a horizontal level actually affects my ability to *believe* and *receive* the glory God wants to pour down in my life and in the life of our church. That's huge. If I participate in our culture's obsession with worshiping other people—even good people like John the Baptist (see John 5:36)—I inhibit the glory of God, which I desperately need.

Where are you in danger of horizontally glorifying other people rather than God?

What can you do to make sure your worship is always focused vertically?

A PRAYER FOR YOU AND ME

In John 17 Jesus prayed an amazing prayer on behalf of His disciples—and they certainly needed it, given what they were about to face. But do you realize Christ added you and me to that prayer as well? That's what He said in Today's Scripture Focus: "I do not ask for these only, but also for those who will believe in me through their word" (v. 20). That's present-day believers.

That means you and I are part of Jesus' request to the Father recorded in verses 22-24:

> *The glory that you have given me I have given to them, that they may*
> *be one even as we are one, I in them and you in me, that they may*
> *become perfectly one, so that the world may know that you sent me*
> *and loved them even as you loved me. Father, I desire that they also,*
> *whom you have given me, may be with me where I am, to see my glory that*
> *you have given me because you loved me before the foundation of the world.*

We don't have to wonder what Christ wants to do in our lives. He wants us to see His glory—to experience His glory, believe, and be changed—and He wants us to show that glory to others.

In what ways can believers see Jesus' glory?

How can believers show Jesus' glory to other people?

I pray all the time that God would answer Jesus' prayer in my life and in the lives of those in my church family. Because if God doesn't reveal His glory in the person of Christ, why exactly am I here, and why do we gather as a church?

I hope you have the same prayer. I also hope you will personally see Christ's glory coming down and impacting your life in ways you can't even imagine.

WHY THE VEIL WAS TORN

TODAY'S SCRIPTURE FOCUS   >

"When Christ appeared as a high priest of the good things that have come, then through the greater and more perfect tent (not made with hands, that is, not of this creation) he entered once for all into the holy places, not by means of the blood of goats and calves but by means of his own blood, thus securing an eternal redemption." Hebrews 9:11-12

Whether or not you realize it, you're used to being restricted in where you can go and what you can do. For example, you can't get very far into an airport terminal if you don't have a boarding pass. And even with a boarding pass, you can't carry so much as a full-sized tube of toothpaste onto the plane. There are restrictions in place.

It's not just the airport, of course. Go into a mall or retail store, and you'll see doors marked Authorized Personnel Only. You can't go there. Drive down a country road, and you'll see signs in front of driveways that read Private Property or No Trespassing. You can't go there either. And think of government buildings and military installations. If you don't have the right clearance, you can't go to any of those.

The ancient Israelites didn't have airports, malls, or government buildings, but they had the tabernacle and the temple. They were almost completely restricted from directly encountering what we've been talking about all week: the glory of God.

What do you already know about the tabernacle and the temple?

What images or ideas come to mind when you think about those structures? Why?

THE VEIL IN PLACE

You can't read very far into the Old Testament without encountering the tabernacle and the temple. Both facilities served as the center of religious life for the Jewish people—the tabernacle first as a temporary structure and then the temple as a permanent building after the Israelites were established in the promised land.

Both the tabernacle and the temple were designed with different levels of access. The everyday people could gather outside both structures to interact with others and to present their sacrifices to the priests. But access to the inside was restricted to the Levites and priests who performed the rituals and maintained the various vessels housed within. At the center of the tabernacle and the temple was a special room called the most holy place, which was almost entirely restricted at all times.

We can learn more about the importance and function of these buildings from the Book of Hebrews.

Read Hebrews 9:1-10. What words, phrases, or images stand out to you in these verses? Why?

Write down a one-sentence definition of the word *holy*.

I hope you're starting to see a common theme developing in today's material. Restriction. Limited access. And probably the best physical representation of that restriction was the veil, or curtain, that separated the most holy place from everything else:

> *You shall make a veil of blue and purple and scarlet yarns and fine twined linen.*
> *It shall be made with cherubim skillfully worked into it. And you shall*
> *hang it on four pillars of acacia overlaid with gold, with hooks of gold,*
> *on four bases of silver. And you shall hang the veil from the clasps,*
> *and bring the ark of the testimony in there within the veil. And the veil*
> *hall separate for you the Holy Place from the Most Holy.* Exodus 26:31-33

What's your reaction to the idea of God's presence being veiled inside an empty room? Why?

The reason the most holy place was so highly restricted was that it contained the ark of the covenant. And the reason the ark of the covenant was so significant was that God chose to manifest His presence, His glory, in that space:

> *You shall make a mercy seat of pure gold. Two cubits and a half shall be its length, and a cubit and a half its breadth. And you shall make two cherubim of gold; of hammered work shall you make them, on the two ends of the mercy seat. ... There I will meet with you, and from above the mercy seat, from between the two cherubim that are on the ark of the testimony, I will speak with you about all that I will give you in commandment for the people of Israel.*
> Exodus 25:17-18,22

God gave detailed instructions for the construction of the tabernacle and the temple, and He made it very clear that the Israelites were to remain separated from His presence. As it said in the passage from Hebrews 9, only the high priest could enter the most holy place, "and he but once a year, and not without taking blood, which he offers for himself and for the unintentional sins of the people" (v. 7).

Why did the Israelites need to be separated from direct encounters with God's glory?

Read the following passages of Scripture and record reasons the Israelites needed to be separated from God's glory.

Leviticus 10:1-3

1 Samuel 6:19-21

2 Samuel 6:5-11

Are you getting the message yet? Restriction. The Israelites were restricted from directly experiencing God's glory, and there were severe consequences for any people brash or foolish enough to force their way into such an encounter.

One of the few exceptions to this restriction was Moses, who made a bold request of God: "Please show me your glory" (Ex. 33:18). Incredibly, his request was granted, and Moses was allowed to see God's goodness pass before him in a physical way. The experience was so powerful that Moses was changed physically: his face literally glowed with the reflected glory of God.

Even so, Moses experienced a restriction of his own. Because the sinful Israelites were afraid to look directly at his glowing face, Moses was forced to wear a veil of his own that separated God's glory from the frightened people.

Read Exodus 34:29-35. What's your reaction to these verses? Why?

Maybe you're thinking, *What does all this have to do with the church?* The answer has everything to do with Jesus and His substitutionary death on the cross for your sins and mine.

THE VEIL TORN DOWN

Jesus' death on the cross was a singularly momentous event in the history of the world—of the universe, really. In fact, the exact instant when Jesus' body perished was literally an earth-shaking event. It was an entirely vertical moment when God accepted His Son's innocent death as the atonement for our sin.

Read Matthew 27:45-54. What emotions do you experience when you read those verses? Why?

How was Jesus' glory displayed even in the moment of His death?

I hope you noticed verse 51: "Behold, the curtain of the temple was torn in two, from top to bottom." Remember what I said earlier about the curtain (or veil) that separated the most holy place from the rest of the world? It was the primary symbol of humanity's restriction from direct encounters with God's glory. And when Jesus fulfilled His work of atonement for our sins, that curtain was torn vertically from top to bottom. It wasn't just ruffled or wrinkled. It wasn't knocked down from the poles that supported it. No, the veil was ripped in half because it was no longer needed.

That's what the author of Hebrews wants us to see when we keep reading in chapter 9:

> *When Christ appeared as a high priest of the good things that have come,*
> *then through the greater and more perfect tent (not made with hands,*
> *that is, not of this creation) he entered once for all into the holy places,*
> *not by means of the blood of goats and calves but by means*
> *of his own blood, thus securing an eternal redemption.* Hebrews 9:11-12

Because of what Jesus did, there was no longer any need for an isolated most holy place on earth. He purchased something better for us with His own blood. And because there was no longer a need for the restricted most holy place, the veil of separation was taken away. Now Jesus gives us access to God's glory and holiness:

> *Since we have confidence to enter the holy places by the blood of Jesus, by the new and living way that he opened for us through the curtain, that is, through his flesh, and since we have a great priest over the house of God, let us draw near with a true heart in full assurance of faith, with our hearts sprinkled clean from an evil conscience and our bodies washed with pure water.* Hebrews 10:19-22

What do these verses teach us about Jesus?

What do the two previous passages mean for those who want to experience God's glory?

Are you hearing the message of restriction in those verses? No! Things have changed. Our situation is different now. And it's all because of Jesus.

Look at what Paul wrote in 2 Corinthians 3:18: "We all, with unveiled face, beholding the glory of the Lord, are being transformed into the same image from one degree of glory to another." Remember how Moses had to veil his face because the people were so terrified of God's glory? No more! The veil is gone, and we are encouraged to "draw near." We are told to approach "in full assurance of faith" (Heb. 10:22) what used to be restricted. We are encouraged to say, like Moses, "Please show me your glory" (Ex. 33:18).

What emotions do you experience when you think about your ability to enter God's presence through the blood of Jesus?

In what ways are you being transformed through fellowship with God?

I hope you've taken advantage of this new opportunity to experience the radiance of God's glory through Jesus Christ. Because I can tell you from my own experience and from the countless experiences of others that it's good. There's no better news than the fact that we have access to God's glorious presence through the sacrifice of Jesus' blood. That's the core of a vertical church.

Day 4 /

WHY THE CHURCH IS HERE

TODAY'S SCRIPTURE FOCUS >

"To him who is able to do far more abundantly than all that we ask or think, according to the power at work within us, to him be glory in the church and in Christ Jesus throughout all generations, forever and ever. Amen." Ephesians 3:20-21

What's your favorite TV show? I know that question may be difficult for some of us to answer because we have a lot of favorite TV shows. But stop and think for a moment. What do you enjoy watching most on television?

Is it a sitcom? A sporting event? A reality show where you get to call in and cast a vote? A drama? A made-for-TV movie on the Oxygen Network? Even if you watch TV only every four years for the summer Olympics, I want you to think about which event you would be most excited to see.

Whenever your favorite TV show is being broadcast over the airways or pumped through electronic cables, it's theoretically available to anyone. The signals being sent out can be accessed by anyone, providing they have the right equipment to receive those signals.

And that's the catch. If you want to watch your favorite TV show, you need to have an access point. Maybe it's a TV with a cable box. Maybe it's an old rabbit-ear antenna. Maybe it's a satellite dish or a smart phone with wireless Internet service. Whatever you choose, there must be something that allows you to capture the electronic signals being sent out before you can experience your favorite show.

There's a similar dynamic at play in the relationship between God's glory and the church.

ACCESSING GOD'S GLORY

I said this earlier, but it bears repeating: there's only one place on earth where God has promised to reveal the glory of His great Son, Jesus Christ, and that's the church. God's revealed glory isn't promised to the Kiwanis Club or to parachurch ministries. It's not promised to universities, seminaries, or private schools.

It's promised to the church. The church is our means of access to the glory of God.

That doesn't mean God's glory is limited in any way. God is omnipresent; He exists everywhere. So His glory is also present everywhere and is reflected in all things. That's why Psalm 19:1 says:

> *The heavens declare the glory of God,*
> *and the sky above proclaims his handiwork.*

How have you seen God's glory revealed in nature?

What emotions do you experience when you see God's glory reflected in His creation?

More importantly, remember that the veil separating God's glory from the rest of us was torn in half at the moment of Jesus' death on the cross. We're no longer restricted from encountering God's glory. Now it's available to us. Now we've been given access.

But just as there needs to be a cable box or an antenna for us to connect with our favorite TV show, God has graciously given us an access point for His glory, and that's the church. Look again at Today's Scripture Focus:

> *To him who is able to do far more abundantly than all that we ask or think,*
> *according to the power at work within us, to him be glory in the church and*
> *in Christ Jesus throughout all generations, forever and ever.* Ephesians 3:20-21

"To Him be glory in the church." That's what this study's all about.

Think about your experiences with church as a child and in recent years. If you could condense those experiences into one word, what would it be? Why?

How have you seen God's glory in the church?

Let me make another clarification. There are church buildings, and then there's the church. When most people hear "the church," they instinctively think about church buildings—physical structures set up in just about every community across North America and throughout most of the world.

In truth, the church is something different. The church isn't made of bricks or concrete or plaster. The church is made of people. It's the entire community of people who've been redeemed by God, all knitted together by the Holy Spirit on the foundation of Jesus Christ:

> *You are no longer strangers and aliens, but you are fellow citizens with the saints and members of the household of God, built on the foundation of the apostles and prophets, Christ Jesus himself being the cornerstone, in whom the whole structure, being joined together, grows into a holy temple in the Lord. In him you also are being built together into a dwelling place for God by the Spirit.*
> Ephesians 2:19-22

What words and phrases stand out to you in these verses? Why?

What do these verses teach you about the church?

Read the following verses and record what each one contributes to your understanding of the church.

1 Corinthians 3:1-16

1 Corinthians 12:12-31

Hebrews 3:1-6

WHAT GOD WANTS TO ACCOMPLISH

Most people who are part of the church have a lot of expectations for what it should accomplish. We want stronger marriages because of church, for example. We want our kids to learn about Christ. We want to be supported and lifted up when we stumble. Church is for evangelism, for healing, for discipleship, sometimes for discipline. I could put a thousand things on that list.

What are some of your expectations for the church? What do you hope to experience by participating in the life of a church?

But here's what we need to understand: all of those things have to be done a certain way in order for the church to function properly. Specifically, they have to be done in a way that gives glory to God.

We don't just do ministry at church. We do ministry in a way that shows off how awesome God is, because the church is the place of Christ's glory.

When that happens, we'll experience what we saw in Today's Scripture Focus: "To [God] who is able to do far more abundantly than all that we ask or think" (Eph. 3:20). I frequently ask my church to repeat the phrase "God is able." But able to do what? More! Much more than we would ever think to ask Him for. Much more than we could even conceive of Him doing.

God has certainly done more in our church than I ever dreamed. More people, more passion, more love for Jesus, more healing and helping and reveling in all He is. Every week I get to experience window-rattling, earth-shattering, life-altering church.

But I still ask for more when I read what Paul wrote next: "According to the power at work within us" (v. 20). The metric for measuring what God wants to do in your church and mine—in your life and mine—is not our ability but His. What can be accomplished is not based on our power but His.

When have you attempted to engage in ministry based on your own power rather than God's? What happened?

When have you experienced a ministry encounter that flowed from God's power rather than your own? What emotions did you experience during and after that encounter?

God wants to do in your church and in your life more than you could ask or imagine, with His infinite power serving as the gauge that will measure what His ability performs. Wow! And why? Because "to him be glory in the church" (v. 21).

The harder part in all this is that God won't do *through* us what He can't do *in* us. It's easy to sit back and wish my church and my attempts at ministry were more vertical, more powerful, more culturally penetrating, and more glorious. But do I want that for my own soul? Will I let God do *in* me what I long to see God do *through* me and those I partner with in the church?

How do you answer those questions?

I pray that God will continue to make you spiritually fit to receive what He's already willing to do in your life and your church. Even as you continue with this study, I pray God will grow your faith to go higher and further in the glory He wants to reveal.

WHY THE CHURCH WILL ALWAYS BE HERE

TODAY'S SCRIPTURE FOCUS >

"Jesus answered him, 'Blessed are you, Simon Bar-jonah! For flesh and blood has not revealed this to you, but my Father who is in heaven. And I tell you, you are Peter, and on this rock I will build my church, and the gates of hell shall not prevail against it. I will give you the keys of the kingdom of heaven, and whatever you bind on earth shall be bound in heaven, and whatever you loose on earth shall be loosed in heaven.' " Matthew 16:17-19

I drive to work almost every day, but I'll never forget one critical morning when I came face-to-face with the possibility of failure in my own soul. It was a terrible time for me personally and a difficult time for our church family. Dark clouds hovered overhead—possible bankruptcy, cancer, family crisis, and more.

As I drove toward our main campus in Elgin, storm clouds were quickly moving in from the horizon, and the winds were picking up force. I remember weeping as I watched the windshield wipers move back and forth, and everything in my flesh wanted to call someone and tell them, "I quit!"

Thankfully, God in His mercy met me powerfully in that car. It started with my tears, and then I found my voice to speak with Him. And then at the top of my lungs, I cried out in prayer to the Lord, "I'm not gonna quit. I'm *not* gonna quit. I'M NOT GONNA QUIT!"

I didn't and I haven't and I won't. And I don't want you to quit either. But I know the only thing that will keep you going is the Holy Spirit stirring afresh your passion to see Jesus' glory revealed in the church where you serve.

Have you ever quit or been severely tempted to quit your ministry in the church? Why?

THE CHURCH WON'T FAIL

Given that you're reading this study, I'm willing to bet you have a passion for the Word of God and the church. So you're probably familiar with this key passage on the church in which Jesus tested the disciples on His true identity:

> *When Jesus came into the district of Caesarea Philippi, he asked his disciples, "Who do people say that the Son of Man is?" And they said, "Some say John the Baptist, others say Elijah, and others Jeremiah or one of the prophets." He said to them, "But who do you say that I am?"* Matthew 16:13-15

Notice that Jesus wasn't content with the disciples turning His question into a multiple-choice quiz. He demanded a specific declaration from His followers. And that's where Peter, who didn't often answer the clue phone when Jesus was talking, catapulted to the head of the class: "Simon Peter replied, 'You are the Christ, the Son of the living God' " (v. 16).

What do you recall about Peter's life and personality?

When was the first time you realized Jesus' true identity? What happened next?

Have you publicly affirmed Jesus' identity in recent months? Why or why not?

Everything we know about Peter from Scripture indicates that his answer wasn't some careful, studied response to the evidence he'd gathered from local experts. Rather, this was a from-the-gut confession of what he'd seen in the trenches. He knew who Jesus was in a way that included but went way beyond the rational. Having daily experienced transcendent glory, Peter could form no other conclusion but that Jesus was the promised Messiah—the Son of the living God.

How have you personally experienced Jesus' glory?

In what ways would you like to experience Jesus more deeply?

In Today's Scripture Focus Jesus commented on both the content of Peter's confession and his means of knowing what he knew:

> *Jesus answered him, "Blessed are you, Simon Bar-jonah! For flesh and blood has not revealed this to you, but my Father who is in heaven. And I tell you, you are Peter, and on this rock I will build my church, and the gates of hell shall not prevail against it."* Matthew 16:17-18

What are the two promises Jesus declared in these verses?

1.

2.

When you read this passage, don't let yourself get caught up in the debate about whether Peter was the first pope and all that mess. The important message is clear: Jesus declared that *He* would build *His* church. And He declared that the gates of hell would never prevail against it.

Satan is a devourer, a sower of discord, a destroyer of everything precious, and the archenemy of Jesus' glory. Incredibly, Satan has freedom from God to do a lot of damage. Even so, this dual promise from Jesus Christ—He will build the church, and the gates of hell will not prevail against it—is an awesome truth to cling to in the toughest trenches of church ministry.

I've been in those trenches, and I suspect you have as well. Every warrior in the body of Christ must realize that the reputation of Jesus Christ and our facilitating the revelation of His glory are the only focus that will get us to the finish line of our ministry in a way that's fruitful and fulfilling.

So be encouraged and join your will with mine in responding to Christ. Yes, the church will be victorious, and Christ will never abandon it—nor will we!

Are you willing to join in that declaration? Why or why not?

THE GLORY OF COMMITMENT

When my wife and I were in seminary in the late 1980s, we began to pray, "God, we'll go anywhere You want us to go, but if You'd allow it, we'd like to pastor one church for our ministry." I'd already been a youth pastor at a church of 200 and a singles pastor at a church of 2,000. And I'd studied enough churches with significant fruitfulness to know that long-tenured senior pastorates were a key ingredient in abundant fruitfulness. I never dreamed of a church with 10,000 people; there was no such thing at the time. My heart was much less for a big place and much more for a God place, a glory place.

Looking back after more than 25 years of ministry at Harvest, I realize we had no idea what we were really asking for when we prayed to stay in one place. Why would any family want one pastor for their whole lives—least of all me—and why would I want them to see my earliest failings and my struggles to overcome them? Why not move to a church on the other side of the country where we could begin afresh in the strength of the lessons learned, away from the gaze of those predicting our demise?

By now you can guess the single-word answer—*glory*. It's the only word that dictates every decision in a vertical church. What brings more glory to Christ: persevering in relationships or starting over? What brings more glory to Christ: running from your failures or staying put and facing up to them in God's strength? What better reflects the glory of Christ: enduring relationships characterized by forgiveness or temporary ones fashioned in the shifting sand of "What can you do for me"?

How do you answer those questions? Why?

Look, I'm not judging you if you've moved around, changed churches, or bounced back and forth between different ministry opportunities. Sometimes we make mistakes—I certainly have—and sometimes we don't have a choice in the matter.

But I want to challenge you to commit to your area of ministry for as long as God wants you to serve. If you've been burned in ministry before and find it difficult to trust again, I understand. Me too. If you're struggling to accept forgiveness because of your own failures, I understand. Me too.

What obstacles hold you back from fully committing to your ministry calling in the church?

What will it take to overcome those obstacles?

In the end it all comes down to this: What will bring the most glory to Jesus? That's the plumb line by which all of your decisions should be measured, especially your participation in church.

What do you need to do in your church to bring more glory to Jesus?

I hope you'll ask yourself that question as we continue to study together what it means to be a vertical church. And I hope you'll commit to your part in revealing the glory of Jesus Christ to the world.

AN EPIC FAILURE

ICHABOD

WEEK FOUR

START

Welcome back to this small-group discussion of *Vertical Church.*

The application challenge from the previous session involved a prayer walk at your church. If you're comfortable, share your experiences, including the focus of your prayers.

What did you like best from week 3 in the workbook? What questions do you still have?

In what ways were the tabernacle and the temple similar to the church today? In what ways is the church different?

What obstacles hold people back from fully participating in the life and ministry of their church?

To prepare to view the DVD segment, read these verses aloud.

> *His daughter-in-law, the wife of Phinehas, was pregnant, about to give birth.*
> *And when she heard the news that the ark of God was captured,*
> *and that her father-in-law and her husband were dead, she bowed*
> *and gave birth, for her pains came upon her. And about the time*
> *of her death the women attending her said to her, "Do not be afraid,*
> *for you have borne a son." But she did not answer or pay attention.*
> *And she named the child Ichabod, saying, "The glory has departed*
> *from Israel!" because the ark of God had been captured and because*
> *of her father-in-law and her husband. And she said, "The glory*
> *has departed from Israel, for the ark of God has been captured."*
> 1 Samuel 4:19-22

WATCH

Complete the viewer guide below as you watch DVD session 4.

An epic failure: _____

When the people of God are not told the _____ of God from the _____ of God, they lose the _____ of God, and everyone does that which is right in his own eyes.

_____ **shepherds: failure to put the people _____**

If you buy into a system, even a Christian system, that is filled with the _____ of men and not the _____ of God, you lose.

_____ **sheep: failure to _____ to established authority**

Nothing causes more heartache for the servants of Christ in a church than people who won't _____.

It's not about you or me. It's about honoring _____ in the church.

_____ **sheep: failure to _____ people the Word of God**

If you place your kids above God, you place them at _____.

_____ **service: failure to _____ _____ sin and deal with it**

Ichabod: always dark because the _____ is gone

We come to church to see the _____ come down.

The church is for _____.

Anything we would do to keep the glory from coming down is epic _____.

RESPOND

Discuss the DVD segment with your group, using the questions below.

> What about the DVD segment was most interesting to you? Why?

> What does our culture think about everyone doing what's right in his own eyes?

> Based on your experiences in today's culture, what are some consequences when everyone does what's right in his own eyes?

> How do you react to this statement? "If you buy into a system, even a Christian system, that is filled with the traditions of men and not the Word of God, you lose."

> What are some human traditions that have made their way into the church?

> Look again at 1 Samuel 4:19-22. What emotions do you experience when you read these verses? Why?

> What emotions do you experience when you think about the decline of the church in North America? What about your community?

APPLICATION

This week conduct research to gain perspective on the current health of the church in North America. You can read a book or blogs, track down statistics online, talk with church leaders, interview church members, and so on.

SCRIPTURE MEMORY FOR THIS WEEK
In those days there was no king in Israel.
Everyone did what was right in his own eyes.
Judges 21:25

READ WEEK 4 AND COMPLETE THE ACTIVITIES BEFORE THE NEXT GROUP EXPERIENCE.

WEEK 4

MEMORY VERSE >

"In those days there was no king in Israel. Everyone did what was right in his own eyes."

Judges 21:25

SAY IT IN A SENTENCE >

When the people of God aren't told the works of God, they lose the wonder of God. Everybody does what's right in their own eyes, and the glory of God departs.

CAN WE HANDLE THE TRUTH? >

"You can't handle the truth!" That was Jack Nicholson's famous cry to Tom Cruise while playing Colonel Nathan R. Jessup in the climactic scene of *A Few Good Men*. I wonder if the screenwriters knew how succinctly they'd summarized our culture in a single sentence. Individual capacity to bear the weight of truth has been mortally wounded in a world that idolizes tolerance and despises anyone who threatens our addiction to autonomy.

If this were only true in society at large, that would be one thing, but as Christian philosopher extraordinaire Francis Schaeffer's book *The Great Evangelical Disaster* made clear, the spirit of the age becomes the spirit of the church. For that reason it's imperative that every church member, leader, and pastor prayerfully evaluate and apply this week's lessons.

I can imagine readers asking, "Why can't you focus on the positives of vertical church without exposing its absence in churches today?" There are several answers to that question.

- Because Paul, Peter, John, and Jesus spoke out against the failures of the church, and their example compels me to do the same
- Because adopting a lowest-common-denominator gospel weakens the body of Christ
- Because no shepherd who's faithful to his calling can be silent when the sheep aren't well fed
- Because the gospel fails when we hide it in a museum to admire rather than unleashing it in the world
- Because the glory of Jesus is at stake, and we can't be passive when He's denied

The bottom line is that the church in North America is failing, and it's been failing for decades. Unless we acknowledge the truth of our condition, we'll never take the necessary steps to become vertical churches that are powerful in God's strength.

UNGODLY LEADERS

TODAY'S SCRIPTURE FOCUS >

"The sin of the young men was very great in the sight of the LORD, for the men treated the offering of the LORD with contempt." 1 Samuel 2:17

Did you notice the title of this week's material? I believe the North American church is in the middle of an epic failure. And when I say epic, I'm not referring to the fact that "we all stumble in many ways" (Jas. 3:2). I'm not talking about a failure like "Oops, we forgot to order supplies."

I'm talking a nuclear meltdown. I'm saying all this stuff we've built up and admired for centuries in and around our churches is beginning to crumble underneath us. And if you don't believe me, take a moment to look at the statistics.
- Six thousand churches close their doors every year.
- Thirty-five hundred Americans leave the church every day.
- Only 1 pastor in 10 retires while still in ministry.
- Fewer than 20 percent of Americans regularly attend church.
- Only 15 percent of churches in the United States are growing numerically.
- Only 2 percent of growing churches are effectively winning converts to Christ.
- Only 9 percent of evangelicals tithe through their churches.
- Only eight hundred new church plants survive each year.
- Ten thousand new churches are needed annually to keep up with population growth.[1]

That's an epic failure.

What's your reaction to those statistics? What surprised you most?

What evidence of this epic failure have you seen in your past experiences with church? What evidence do you see in your current city or community?

I don't know about the church in China, Australia, or South America. But I feel a sense of responsibility for the church in North America—the church I've been connected with all my life. This failure is happening on my watch—and yours.

That being said, I know it's difficult to diagnose our own selfishness and failures. So we're going to dive into 1 Samuel to identify some parallels with our own situations. But first some context.

THE ROOT OF FAILURE

After Moses led the Israelites out of Egypt and through the wilderness and Joshua led them into the promised land, God appointed several regional judges to govern and lead the people spiritually as they dispersed by tribe throughout the land. These leaders were often successful in a military sense, driving out their enemies and further securing portions of the land. But when it came to spiritual leadership, they scored a zero.

Read Judges 2:11-23. What strikes you as most interesting in these verses? Why?

In your own words, summarize what the Israelites experienced under the judges' leadership.

Judges 21:25, the last verse in the book, perfectly summarizes the situation: "In those days there was no king in Israel. Everyone did what was right in his own eyes." The Israelites forgot that God was King, and so they made themselves kings.

The parallels between the time of the judges and the North American church are apparent and troubling. So many of us don't consult the oracles of God when we plan our ministry and service; instead, we do whatever seems right in our own eyes. And what we choose to do is usually couched in the horizontal language of business. Too often churches use leadership techniques, human-centered strategy, and entrepreneurship to reach consumers instead of applying biblical principles to make disciples.

SELFISH SHEPHERDS

In 1 Samuel we're going to look at the lives and "ministry" of two men, Hophni and Phinehas, who served as shepherds of God's people in the city of Shiloh. Here's how they're introduced in 1 Samuel 2:12: "The sons of Eli were worthless men." The second thing we learn about them is even more damning: "They did not know the LORD."

Intrigued? Keep reading this disturbing passage of Scripture, which ends with Today's Scripture Focus.

Read 1 Samuel 2:12-17. How would you summarize the actions and attitudes of Eli's sons?

Read Leviticus 3:3-5. What do these verses say about their actions and attitudes?

In Eli's day the detailed instructions from the books of Moses had been replaced by traditions and customs that blended God's law with pagan rituals the people had witnessed while conquering the promised land. Instead of following God's Word, they were making up their jobs as they went along. So instead of being content with the portions of the sacrifices God had specified for them and waiting for the preparations to be completed, Hophni and Phinehas took what they wanted when they wanted it.

Notice the people still remembered that the fat belonged to God, but they were overruled by selfish shepherds who disregarded God's command for personal gain. This problem is rampant in the church today. So-called prosperity preachers have built a false theology around a lavish lifestyle by pilfering from those in poverty in the name of God.

Even more frightening is the way Eli's sons slipped from taking more than their share materially to taking what was not theirs morally.

Read 1 Samuel 2:22-25. How do these verses support the text's claim that Eli's sons were "worthless men" (v. 2)?

When was the last time you heard about a pastor or church leader committing a moral failure? What was the fallout in the church?

Eli and his sons were blind to the way their selfish acts were affecting the worshipers in their care. Unfortunately, the same is true of many church leaders today. Here's a quick look at some of the ways selfish shepherds continue to harm the church.
- Taking more salary, time, or leisure than is rightly theirs for their labor
- Expecting grace and forgiveness from others when they don't reciprocate
- Treating ministry as a right to be perpetuated instead of a privilege to be appreciated
- Refusing the correction of other elders or leaders while insisting their colleagues be accountable
- Leading at a distance by using people to get the work done but not loving them deeply
- Stealing the thoughts of others rather than stoking their passion for Christ with originality
- Demanding privilege appropriate to their position instead of accepting the role of a servant

Which of these harmful practices have you tolerated—or are tolerating now—in your church?

What steps can you take to prevent these practices?

STUBBORN SHEEP

So that we won't place all the blame for the failures of a church at the feet of its leaders, we need to acknowledge the existence of stubborn sheep. In any congregation you'll find a number of members who refuse to submit to church leaders' authority, refuse to be held accountable for their shortcomings, spread poison throughout the community, and more.

Read the following passages of Scripture and record what each one communicates about the character and behavior of stubborn sheep.

Ezekiel 3:4-11

Acts 5:1-11

1 Corinthians 1:10-17

There will always be sons of Eli—both leaders and lay people who try to dishonor the Lord in order to advance themselves. When we allow that to happen unchallenged, we put the glory of God at risk. God will quickly withdraw His favor where sin is ignored or avoided and where difficult people are coddled instead of confronted in love.

How sad when church leaders say, "We'll just deal with it by living with it. We'll just leave that alone and form a plan to compensate for that callousness." A vertical church confronts stubborn sheep and refuses to fall into shallow service that dishonors God.

Are you functioning as a stubborn sheep in any way? If so, what can you do about it?

How are you enabling the presence of stubborn sheep in your church? What steps can you take in the near future to address the problems they create?

In the end vertical church is never about any individual or even any leader. It's about the glory of God. It's about honoring God in the church so that nobody earns favoritism or special treatment that puts the church at risk of dishonoring the Lord. May it be so for you and your church this week and in the future.

GLORY DEPARTED

TODAY'S SCRIPTURE FOCUS >

"About the time of her death the women attending her said to her, 'Do not be afraid, for you have borne a son.' But she did not answer or pay attention. And she named the child Ichabod, saying, 'The glory has departed from Israel!' because the ark of God had been captured and because of her father-in-law and her husband. And she said, 'The glory has departed from Israel, for the ark of God has been captured.' " 1 Samuel 4:20-22

We've already experienced some haunting passages of Scripture this week. Judges 21:25 is one example: "In those days there was no king in Israel. Everyone did what was right in his own eyes." First Samuel 2:12 is another: "The sons of Eli were worthless men. They did not know the LORD."

Similarly, 1 Samuel 3:1 provides another distressing commentary on spiritual leadership in Eli's day: "The boy Samuel was ministering to the LORD in the presence of Eli. And the word of the LORD was rare in those days; there was no frequent vision."

Of the three verses mentioned, which do you find most troubling? Why?

What do the three verses have in common?

The people of Eli's day were coming to the house of God, but they weren't hearing from Him. They were starving sheep, and the consequences were spiritually deadly. Without the sanctifying regularity of exposure to the Scriptures, the people of God lost the wonder of God's revealed glory, and everyone started doing what was right in their own eyes.

I'm dismayed by the number of pastors in Christian churches who stand up in the pulpit with barely a scrap of Scripture and wax eloquent for 30 minutes without speaking for God. Five funny stories or smiley platitudes, six "It seems to me" statements, and "Three things I've always wanted to talk about" may lead to kudos at the church door from members with itchy ears. I understand that. But what's God's take on those sermons? How does God view such talks when His Word isn't heralded? Here's the reality: if God hasn't revealed it, it has no power.

Today we're going to wrap up the story of Eli and his sons by focusing on two passages of Scripture and exploring two implications for Christians and the church.

WHO NEEDS WHOM?

For those of us who are dedicated to serving and glorifying God through His church—both pastors and lay people—things begin to unravel when we start feeling that the church needs us in order to function properly. Or even worse, that God needs us in order to accomplish anything worthwhile in the world.

It's the other way around, of course, which is a message Jesus communicated in His ministry.

Read Luke 17:7-10. What was the main idea Jesus communicated in these verses?

What's your reaction to that idea? Why?

As we saw yesterday, Eli and his two sons lost their sense of perspective on their positions as spiritual leaders among God's people. It didn't take long for God to remind them who was actually in charge.

Read 1 Samuel 2:27-36. What words or phrases stand out to you in these verses? Why?

What was the primary message the "man of God" (v. 27) delivered?

What were the specific offenses Eli and his sons had committed?

We've already seen that Hophni and Phinehas were "worthless men" (v. 12), so let's take a look at how the man of God highlighted Eli's mistakes.

First, God told Eli, "You … honor your sons above me" (v. 29). That verse should be underlined in every person's Bible—especially every pastor's Bible. If the loud demands of a few become more important than God's reputation, that's a problem. Indeed, when we place people above God, we put them at risk and become complicit in their sin.

This is a major problem today in the Western church. How many services next Sunday have already been designed according to people's shallow needs or desires instead of what God commands in His Word and endorses with His presence?

When are you tempted to place the needs of other people above God and His glory?

Second, God highlighted Eli's belief that he was somehow special and vital to God's work with the people of Israel. Eli was a descendent of Aaron, the first high priest, and God had promised that Aaron's descendents would continue to minister in His house forever. Therefore, Eli thought his place in ministry, along with the place of his sons, would always be secure.

Eli was wrong. God said, "Those who honor me I will honor, and those who despise me shall be lightly esteemed" (v. 30). Other descendents of Aaron could serve in the tabernacle, just as many other Christians today can be used to reveal God's glory in the church and in the world if we don't uphold our responsibility.

When are you tempted to feel prideful about your work and ministry in the church?

How can you maintain a proper perspective on your value in comparison to God's?

ICHABOD

Not only did Eli and his family carry a false sense of security about their role as spiritual leaders, but they also had an outrageously misguided belief in their ability to understand and control God's manifest presence—His glory revealed in the community.

In 1 Samuel 4 Israel went to battle against its archenemy, the Philistines. And things didn't go well from the start: "Israel was defeated before the Philistines, who killed about four thousand men on the field of battle" (v. 2). That's when Hophni and Phinehas, who were leading the show, had a bright idea: "Let us bring the ark of the covenant of the LORD here from Shiloh, that it may come among us and save us from the power of our enemies" (v. 3).

Notice that God was an afterthought: *Wow, we're getting hammered. Maybe we better go back and get God involved.* And at first their plan seemed to work. The Israelites gave a mighty shout when they saw the ark, and the Philistines became afraid. But then everything collapsed.

Read 1 Samuel 4:10-18. Were you surprised when you read verses 10-11? Why or why not?

How do these verses fulfill God's promises spoken by the "man of God" in 1 Samuel 2:27?

Read 1 Samuel 5:1-12. What do these verses teach us about God?

Notice that when Eli heard what had happened, what sent shockwaves through his brain wasn't the death of his sons but the news that the ark had been captured. It's difficult for us to comprehend today just what that news meant. At that time the ark of God was the place of His presence—where God's glory came down. How could the godless Philistines have captured it?

However, God's message was clear: His glory isn't at our whim. He alone decides when to manifest His presence, and He reserves the right to remove that presence whenever He finds it necessary.

That's evident in Today's Scripture Focus. When Phinehas's wife learned about all that had happened, her grief was so great that she went into labor. And in a terribly poignant gesture of despair, she captured what so many people continue to miss about the absence of God's glory among His people:

> *About the time of her death the women attending her said to her, "Do not be afraid, for you have borne a son." But she did not answer or pay attention. And she named the child Ichabod, saying, "The glory has departed from Israel!"*
> 1 Samuel 4:20-21

Please hear the message shouted by that young woman and her son: you don't hold a monopoly on God's glory. God wasn't bound to manifest His presence in the ark, and He isn't bound to manifest His presence or display His glory in any church—including yours.

In fact, if you contribute to horizontal methods of ministry and a human-pleasing, glory-stealing atmosphere in your community of worship, God will depart from you. He will withdraw His glory.

What's your reaction to the previous statements? Why?

How can you determine whether God has declared "Ichabod" in your church or ministry?

If God's glory has departed, what steps can you take to repent and seek His presence again?

Day 3 /

APPALLING AND HORRIBLE

TODAY'S SCRIPTURE FOCUS   >

"An appalling and horrible thing

has happened in the land:

the prophets prophesy falsely,

and the priests rule at their direction;

my people love to have it so,

but what will you do when the end comes?" Jeremiah 5:30-31

Have you noticed how hard pharmaceutical companies work to disguise the taste of medicine these days? Flu remedies are now powdered so that we can place them in hot water and pretend we're drinking tea. Cold remedies come in gelcaps, which feature a layer of dissolvable plastic that shields your taste buds from the medicine. Or sometimes a pill comes with a coating of sugar that gives you a sweet sensation as you swallow.

But here's the reality: medicine tastes bad. It's unpleasant. But we must be willing to endure that unpleasantness if we want to receive the benefits.

I hope you're willing to continue diving into the unpleasant reality of Ichabod as it applies to the church in North America today. Because as we work to understand our failures and where things have gone wrong, we give ourselves a better chance at healing.

What emotions have you experienced while studying this material over the past two days?

What do you hope to learn or experience with the material yet to come?

As church members and leaders, we need to understand that certain attitudes and practices invite, promote, and encourage the manifest presence of God and His glory to come down in our midst. We've talked about some of those things already, and we'll continue to focus on practical action steps we can take. That's important.

But other actions and attitudes grieve the Spirit of God and wound the movement of God in church. There are things we do that push against God's manifest presence, ultimately resulting in Ichabod— God's glory departing from the church.

Over the next three days we'll examine words of the prophet Jeremiah as we explore several reasons God's glory has departed from the Western church.

MISSING THE MARK

Yesterday we finished examining the epic failure of God's leaders and God's people as described in the Book of 1 Samuel, along with ways that failure is paralleled in the North American church today. In a similar way, I want to explore another period of failure for God's people.

We'll start with Today's Scripture Focus:

> *An appalling and horrible thing*
> *has happened in the land:*
> *the prophets prophesy falsely,*
> *and the priests rule at their direction;*
> *my people love to have it so,*
> *but what will you do when the end comes?* Jeremiah 5:30-31

What words and phrases stand out to you in those verses? Why?

How would you summarize the "appalling and horrible thing" (v. 30) in your own words?

As a prophet called by God, Jeremiah spoke the words of God. Through Jeremiah, God continually warned His people about their coming doom at the hand of Nebuchadnezzar and the Babylonians, but the people repeatedly chose not to listen. Why? Because other prophets had chosen to "prophesy falsely" (v. 31). They claimed to speak for God, as Jeremiah did, but they substituted their own messages instead of communicating the dire warning God wanted to deliver.

Even worse, "the priests rule at their direction" (v. 31). Here's how it worked in the Old Testament. The prophets proclaimed God's Word, and the priests were responsible to teach and administrate worship among the people. In Jeremiah's day, however, the priests mimicked false prophets by ruling in their own authority rather than God's. They weren't calling on God, they weren't studying the Scriptures, and they weren't seeking wise counsel. They were doing whatever they thought best.

How can you recognize when people proclaim their own ideas in church today rather than speaking what God places on their hearts from His Word?

When have you made spiritual decisions based on your own wisdom and authority rather than God's? What happened?

Worst of all, God said, "My people love to have it so" (v. 31). The Israelites didn't want to hear what Jeremiah had to say; they didn't want to hear about judgment and the coming consequences of their sin. They wanted to keep things rolling along smoothly so that they could maintain their religious grooves without changing the defective elements in their lives. This is horizontal religion at its worst. People find it easy to get along or ignore human-centered, human-generated religion. God's Word provokes either rejection or repentance.

Do your experiences with church cause you to feel conviction about the defective areas of your life? Why or why not?

Read 2 Timothy 4:1-4. How is this similar to Today's Scripture Focus, Jeremiah 5:30-31?

Refusing to accurately proclaim God's Word and refusing to hear when God's Word is proclaimed are two reasons God's glory departs from His people. But there are many others. Let's explore some.

PLACING SOTERIOLOGY ABOVE DOXOLOGY

Are you ready for some vocabulary words? *Soteriology* is a word that comes from the Greek word *soterios,* which means *to save.* Therefore, soteriology is the doctrine of salvation in Jesus Christ, or the study of how people become saved. It reflects a focus on evangelism, which is certainly a good thing in a church.

But evangelism isn't our primary purpose. Our most important pursuit can be called *doxology,* which comes from the Greek word translated *glory.* As followers of Jesus, as members of His church, we have a primary goal that's best described as doxological: we're here to glorify God. The first and most important questions in our lives and in our churches should always be: Does that honor God? Does that honor His Word? Does that honor His Son?

How would you describe soteriology in your own words?

How would you describe doxology in your own words?

Based on the previous weeks of study, why do you think doxology is the primary mission of believers and churches?

Placing an evangelistic goal above the mission of God's glory is an incredibly destructive error in the church today—one from which many other errors fall out. When we desire to reach people more than we desire to glorify God, we grieve the Holy Spirit and forfeit God's manifest presence.

Why? Because what starts as a desire to see people added to the kingdom of God eventually morphs into a desire to see people added to *our* church specifically. We want numerical growth; we want more and more people in our church buildings. So we alter and compromise the gospel to make it palatable for more and more people.

In the end we begin to mirror these words from Jeremiah: "From the least to the greatest of them, everyone is greedy for unjust gain; and from prophet to priest, everyone deals falsely" (Jer. 6:13).

How can a desire for more church members cause church leaders to become "greedy for unjust gain"?

If the greatest desire in your life and your church is to glorify God, you'll experience His presence and find ample opportunities to reach people with the gospel. But when you allow your focus to drift horizontally—when you take your eyes away from God and focus on people instead—you're in trouble.

PLACING RELEVANCE ABOVE TRANSCENDENCE

In a similar way, many church leaders begin to focus on relevance in the culture rather than on transcendence, the awesomeness of God and His glory. Jeremiah 6:10 says:

Behold, the word of the LORD is to them an object of scorn;
they take no pleasure in it.

How many people do you know who are offended by the Word of God? Have you ever seen churches try to soften the message of the Bible to make it more appealing to those who would be offended? Have you ever seen churches and pastors perform crazy stunts in an effort to appear cool rather than clearly and honestly proclaiming what God says in His Word?

How would you answer the previous questions?

When have you felt offended by God's Word? How did you respond?

If we build our churches on celebrity guests and circus chicanery of all sorts, we'll attract the kind of people who want shallow service, and we'll grow them into snotty-nosed, high-demand, never-satisfied "disciples." Good luck with that.

What are some ways churches can compromise the truth of God's Word by trying to be relevant?

How can Christians be relevant in today's culture without sacrificing the transcendence and truth of God's Word?

On the other hand, if we build our churches on a hunger for transcendent encounters with the holiness of God, we'll grow Word-centered, passionate followers of God's great Son, Jesus Christ. True disciples can take any hill on any day without complaining, because they know life isn't about them.

I know which of those options I want for myself, and I know which one I want for my church. What about you?

PEACE, PEACE

TODAY'S SCRIPTURE FOCUS >

"They have healed the wound of my people lightly, saying, 'Peace, peace,' when there is no peace." Jeremiah 6:14

Do you know the sound big trucks make when they operate in reverse? "Beep, beep, beep." Play that sound in your mind right now because I want to back up for a few moments before we move forward again with today's material.

Yesterday we talked about two errors that have contributed to the departure of God's glory from the North American church: placing soteriology above doxology and placing relevance before transcendence. I firmly believe many churches today have made these mistakes, and I'm convinced those mistakes have contributed to the epic failure we're currently experiencing in the body of Christ.

But I don't want to give you the impression that soteriology and relevance are bad—that they're harmful in and of themselves. That's not the case. Rather, they're good things that cause damage only when they keep us from focusing on what's best: showing forth God's glory in the world.

Jesus helped us understand this reality when He said:

> *You shall love the Lord your God with all your heart and with all your soul and with all your mind. This is the great and first commandment. And a second is like it: You shall love your neighbor as yourself. On these two commandments depend all the Law and the Prophets.* Matthew 22:37-40

Do you see the progression? Loving our neighbor is crucial as individual Christians and as churches. It's the second most important thing we can do. Yet we must always direct our energy *first* at loving and glorifying God. When we love God with everything we have, we'll be in the best position possible to love our neighbors also. But when we reverse those priorities, we lose both.

What are some good things that have obstructed your efforts to love God first?

What are practical ways you can submit those good things to your love of God? Today we'll look at two more ways a horizontal concern for people has obstructed our vertical priorities as individual believers and as churches.

PLACING HELP BEFORE HOLINESS

In the middle of his devastating indictment of the failures of the spiritual leaders in Jerusalem, Jeremiah shared God's observation recorded in Today's Scripture Focus:

> **They have healed the wound of my people lightly,**
> **saying, "Peace, peace," when there is no peace.** Jeremiah 6:14

I don't know about you, but when people come to our church for the first time, they almost always come carrying a basket with something broken in it: "Our marriage is falling apart." "My job is gone." "Our former church lost its shepherd." They don't come with little scratches or bruises; they come with missing body parts. Emotionally, mentally, and spiritually, they're coming apart. And they're saying, "Help me." "Heal me." "Minister to me." "Save me."

When have you come to church carrying something broken? Did you experience the healing you were looking for?

Who has recently come to your church in search of help and healing? What have they received?

That's how it's always been, and that's how it was in ancient Jerusalem. But according to Jeremiah, God's verdict was that false prophets and false servants had "healed the wound of my people lightly." In other words, they were trying to use a bandage to treat gangrene. They said, " 'Peace, Peace,' when there is no peace." The spiritual doctors were deliberately falsifying the diagnosis so that the patient wouldn't be scared.

I believe the same thing is happening today. So many times sermons are reduced to little pep talks: "Hey, get on top of it. You're not supposed to be under it; you're supposed to be over it. You're not the tail; you're the head!" Really? That's all you've got?

Church has to be more than an emotional shot in the arm. Sermons have to be more than a lightly psychological motivational speech. People can find that every day on "Dr. Phil." Worship must be an encounter with the God of the universe. It has to be personal, crisis-causing, life-transforming, Holy Spirit-led, and moving! That's when people find healing.

When have you received pep talks and/or pop psychology from church leaders? What emotions did you experience at the time?

Have you recently said "Peace, peace" to hurting people? If so, what happened next?

What's the best way to help hurting people? That's the basic question underlying this conversation. When people come into our lives or into the church with wounds and soul-crushing problems, what's the best way to serve them? How do we take care of them in a way that brings lasting healing?

Once again, we find the answer in Jesus' life and ministry.

Read Mark 2:1-12. What were the primary problems experienced by the paralytic?

What can we learn from Jesus' decision to address the man's spiritual condition before his physical condition?

Jesus was more interested in the man's holiness than in his paralysis. And it was only after He forgave the man's sins that He also addressed his physical ailment. We must follow the same priorities in church.

One symptom of misguided priorities is our current overemphasis or overdependence on grace. Now thank God for grace. I hope you sense an undercurrent of grace in everything we explore in this study. I hope you hear the message that no matter where you've been or what you've been, God loves you, and He reaches out to you in His Son, Jesus Christ.

But God doesn't want to leave you where you are, and He doesn't just want to forgive you. He wants to change your life. That's why we need to move from just teaching the gospel of grace to teaching the gospel of holiness: God wants you to be transformed from glory to glory as a demonstration of His saving power (see 2 Cor. 3:18). Too many people claim to be running the marathon race of Christian holiness, but they seem to spend most of their time at the water station of grace instead of taking strides toward the finish line.

What does it mean to be holy?

How do we become holy as followers of Jesus?

One problem is that many people and churches view holiness like stale medicine with cod-liver oil: "Here, eat this. It tastes terrible, but it'll do wonders for you!" That's not the case with holiness.

Holiness is the best thing God has to give you. Holiness is the character of God, and it's what you desperately need. It's because of an absence of holiness that you've been so restless and miserable for so long. To get just a taste of who God is and to be done once and for all with yourself and all your selfishness and silliness—that's holiness. If we only believed that, we'd understand why Scripture teaches so much about holiness and why God Himself said, "Be holy, for I am holy" (1 Pet. 1:16).

We have to desire holiness above help.

PLACING THE THERAPEUTIC BEFORE THE GOSPEL

There's another danger that flows from the healing-wounds-lightly approach. Too many of us are offering a therapeutic gospel before and sometimes instead of the life-changing gospel of Jesus Christ. We're practicing a shallow compassion that addresses only felt needs rather than applying the costly compassion of the gospel that addresses transcendent needs.

You see this tendency in Christian bookstores all the time: *Five Easy Steps to a Better Marriage, Three Ways to Communicate at Work, Four Things to Teach Your Kids Before They Turn 5,* and so on. There's value in those messages as long as they grow from Scripture. But when we encourage people to determine how God will help them rather than leading them to surrender to God Himself, we leave them in control of their lives, severely limiting their experience with God.

In your own words, what does it mean to place therapeutic or self-help concerns before the gospel of Jesus?

What does the gospel offer that therapeutic assistance can't?

The standard invitation in New Testament preaching was "Repent." It wasn't "God's anxious to do something really cool for you that you'll like."

Read the following passages of Scripture and record what they teach about repentance.

Luke 13:1-5

2 Corinthians 7:8-13

James 4:1-10

The presentation of the gospel in vertical churches should come in the context of wholehearted worship, where God's glory is so apparent that sinners are profoundly convicted of the distance between themselves and the glory they sense all around them. Their individual needs will fade into insignificance when their need for God Himself is exposed.

I pray that your experiences with the gospel and our presentations of the gospel won't be centered on superficial and temporal needs. Rather, we're called to live the gospel of Jesus. Boldly declare through your words and actions that you've accepted the gift of forgiveness and the blessing of eternal life bathed in the glory of God.

THE TRUTH

TODAY'S SCRIPTURE FOCUS >

"Thus says the LORD:

'Stand by the roads, and look,

and ask for the ancient paths,

where the good way is; and walk in it,

and find rest for your souls.

But they said, "We will not walk in it."

I set watchmen over you, saying,

"Pay attention to the sound of the trumpet!"

But they said, "We will not pay attention." ' " Jeremiah 6:16-17

A number of tips and tricks can help people become more relaxed and be more effective in public speaking. It's important that speakers know their material, for example—that they have a thorough understanding of what they want to say and why they want to say it. Rehearsing is another helpful tip. A lot of new speakers try to wing it based on an outline, and they usually end up crashing hard.

Here's another piece of advice that's often offered to public speakers: know your audience, especially the felt needs or other desires that have compelled people to listen to you speak. Because if you tell your audience what they want to hear, you'll come away with pats on the back no matter how badly your presentation falls apart.

There's no doubt that's an effective technique at high-school pep rallies: "Our team's gonna win this Friday!" It's very effective on the campaign trail: "Here are five things I'm going to accomplish during my first year in office."

Telling people what they want to hear, however, is devastating in your personal witness for the gospel, and it's a key element in the epic failure currently afflicting the church.

What do people usually want to hear about their goals in life and the way they live?

What do people want to hear when they come to church?

What do you want to hear from God's Word and your church?

This week we've explored several misguided priorities in the church today.
- Many leaders in the body of Christ have erroneously placed the doctrine of salvation above the church's responsibility to glorify God.
- They've placed being relevant above experiencing the transcendent.
- They've made helping people more important than developing holiness in those people.
- They've decided to be therapeutic in treating people's problems rather than focusing on the gospel of Jesus Christ.

In your opinion, which of those misguided priorities are the most damaging in a church? Why?

About which of those misguided priorities have you been convicted this week?

PLACING COMPASSION BEFORE THE GOSPEL

Another misguided priority afflicting the North American church today stems from telling people what they want to hear rather than telling them what God has to say. And it happens under the guise of showing compassion.

Once again, I need to point out that compassion is important. In my life and in our church, we regularly pray about how we can grow in compassion, including ministering to widows, orphans, and the poor. These are biblically directed priorities (see Jas. 1:27). They're important. But matters of importance can't become matters of first importance.

Let's look at what we can learn about our priorities from Jesus' life and ministry.

Read Mark 6:30-44. What strikes you as most interesting in these verses? Why?

How does this story demonstrate Jesus' compassion?

Most people are familiar with the story of Jesus feeding the five thousand, and it's often presented as evidence that the church should meet the needs of people in the community. After all, Jesus miraculously blessed them with food rather than sending everyone away to fend for themselves. That's true, and that was a wonderful thing.

But look what came first: "When he went ashore he saw a great crowd, and he had compassion on them, because they were like sheep without a shepherd. And he began to teach them many things" (v. 34). Yes, Jesus had compassion on the needs of the crowd, but His first act in response to that compassion was to teach them the good news of His gospel.

Many Christians and churches slip when they place compassionately meeting the needs of people above proclaiming the gospel. They say, "People are walking away from the church, but they still have great physical and emotional needs. We need to change our message so that they'll stop walking away. We need to stop talking about the penalty for sin, the reality of God's judgment, and the demands of following Christ. We need to be nicer so that we'll have the opportunity to show them compassion."

As Christians in North America, we worship at the altar of niceness. And we become hesitant about saying anything to contradict anyone because our God has become the God of relational sweetness, kindness, and niceness—and we bow before that.

How have you seen churches elevate niceness and compassion above the gospel?

When have you felt pressure to deemphasize the message of the gospel to appear more welcoming and kind? What happened?

The truth is, we're responsible for what we present and how we present it, but we're not responsible for the response. Jesus said, "Blessed are you when others revile you and persecute you and utter all kinds of evil against you falsely on my account. Rejoice and be glad, for your reward is great in heaven, for so they persecuted the prophets who were before you" (Matt. 5:11-12).

Jesus was rejected, and He said we will be also. If we're unwilling to take that risk, we're in danger of softening the gospel message. We risk becoming unfaithful to our primary calling to pass on the good news about Jesus.

Read 1 Peter 3:13-17. Are you prepared to "make a defense" (v. 15) for what you believe? Why or why not?

When have you been slandered in the past for the sake of the gospel? How did you respond?

In what ways do you think churches need to be more forthright about presenting the truth of the gospel?

PLACING RELATIONSHIPS BEFORE TRUTH

Another misguided priority that's killing the North American church is our propensity to place value on relationships over truth, and I'm talking largely about relationships that already exist in the church.

Look again at Today's Scripture Focus:

> *Thus says the LORD:*
> *"Stand by the roads, and look,*
> *and ask for the ancient paths,*
> *where the good way is; and walk in it,*
> *and find rest for your souls.*
> *But they said, 'We will not walk in it.'*
> *I set watchmen over you, saying,*
> *'Pay attention to the sound of the trumpet!'*
> *But they said, 'We will not pay attention.' "* Jeremiah 6:16-17

Through Jeremiah, God was telling the people to find the old ways the Israelites had honored Him and then to "walk in it" (v. 16). But the people refused. God sent watchmen to encourage them further—prophets to show the right way and declare God's will. But the people again refused to listen or change their values. Eventually, they experienced devastation.

The same is true in churches today. There are sheep in our flocks who refuse to walk in the way Jesus commanded us to walk, and sadly, there are a number of shepherds who've made the same refusals. So what do we do next? How do we address those sheep?

The Bible tells us what to do.

Read the following passages of Scripture and record what they communicate about church discipline.

Matthew 18:15-20

1 Corinthians 5:1-8

Hebrews 10:19-31

What are some issues and values that need to be confronted in churches today?

Church discipline should be a legitimate part of church life. But often church leaders begin to prioritize relationships over the truth of God's Word. We want to please people. We want to be nice. We don't want to judge.

Even worse, many churches develop certain rules for certain people. They say, "This person is living in sin, and we need to deal with that. But we're going to overlook what that person is doing. That person puts a big check in the offering. That person goes golfing with the pastor every Monday afternoon. So we're going to look the other way."

That's a bad plan.

Read James 2:1-13. What's the primary message of these verses?

When have you been tempted to treat certain people differently because of your relationships with them? What happened?

How can you avoid contributing to a misguided prioritization of relationships over truth in your church? How can you highlight that priority if it exists?

Ichabod. The glory has departed. It's a difficult subject, and I know this has been a difficult week of study as you've examined your heart and the ministry of your church. But it's necessary. The truth isn't always easy or fun, but it's what we really need. And here's the good news, directly from the lips of Jesus: "I will build my church, and the gates of hell shall not prevail against it" (Matt. 16:18).

To reverse the epic failure afflicting churches in North America, those churches must return to a vertical focus. Only God Himself, welcomed back to the place of prominence in His church—only the revealed glory of Jesus in every house of worship—can usher in a new day. And we're going to spend the second half of this study exploring how that can happen.

1. Rebecca Barnes and Lindy Lowry, "Special Report: The American Church in Crisis," Center for Missional Research [cited 11 June 2012]. Available from the Internet: *http://www.namb.net.*

WHAT BRINGS THE GLORY DOWN

UNASHAMED ADORATION

WEEK FIVE

START

Welcome back to this small-group discussion of *Vertical Church.*

The application challenge from the previous session involved doing research on the current health of the North American church. What did you find?

How have you contributed to the health of your local church?

What did you like best from week 4 in the workbook? What questions do you still have?

How can local churches maintain a healthy balance between making the gospel the primary priority yet also remaining relevant and helping those in need?

To prepare to view the DVD segment, read these verses aloud.

> *The priests could not enter the house of the LORD, because the glory of the LORD filled the LORD's house. When all the people of Israel saw the fire come down and the glory of the LORD on the temple, they bowed down with their faces to the ground on the pavement and worshiped and gave thanks to the LORD, saying, "For he is good, for his steadfast love endures forever."*
> 2 Chronicles 7:2-3

WATCH

Complete the viewer guide below as you watch DVD session 5.

The _____ of worship

Worship: to ascribe _____

Worship requires _____.

God is not the sum total of my _____.

Understanding leads to _____.

The _____ of worship

God wants to be worshiped _____.

The _____ of worship

We worship God with our mind when we allow God's thoughts to shape our _____.

God must be worshiped with our _____.

Your _____ enables you to listen and focus as you worship.

THINGS THAT MAKE WORSHIP POWERFUL

1. Worship brings _____ _____.
   Jesus Christ is given His rightful place. He is _____ on the praises of His people.
2. Worship brings _____.
3. Worship brings _____.
4. Worship brings _____.

The _____ of worship

Worship with your _____.

Worship with your _____ and _____.

Worship with your _____.

RESPOND

Discuss the DVD segment with your group, using the questions below.

> What did you like best about the DVD segment? Why?

> What words or images come to your mind when you hear the term *worship*? Why?

> Describe your ideal worship experience in church. What would happen, and what wouldn't happen?

> What's the primary goal of personal worship? What about corporate worship?

> When do you most often experience God's presence during worship?

> How do we worship God with our minds? Our emotions? Our wills?

Work together as a group to develop a list of activities, methods, and practices that followers of Jesus can use to worship Him.

APPLICATION

Identify one activity you can remove from your daily routine this week and replace with a time of worship. For example, take a half-hour break from watching TV and worship God instead. Or listen to a worship CD during your daily commute rather than to talk radio.

SCRIPTURE MEMORY FOR THIS WEEK
God is spirit, and those who worship him must worship in spirit and truth.
John 4:24

READ WEEK 5 AND COMPLETE THE ACTIVITIES BEFORE THE NEXT GROUP EXPERIENCE.

WEEK 5

MEMORY VERSE   >

"God is spirit, and those who worship him must worship in spirit and truth."

John 4:24

SAY IT IN A SENTENCE   >

God's Son, fervently worshiped in spirit and truth, brings glory down in a church.

MISGUIDED ADORATION   >

I'm not a historian, but I've long been fascinated by the Second World War. Specifically, I've studied the gradual ascendancy that led to Adolf Hitler's iron-fisted control of Germany. Inflaming a common hatred of the Jews, carrying out random raids, conducting relentless surveillance, and beating or imprisoning all opponents were the major factors in Hitler's meteoric rise to absolute power.

William Dodd, the American ambassador to Germany, continually warned President Roosevelt, but most world leaders preferred a version of "facts" that discredited reports of Nazi insanity. They wanted to avoid another great war. But another cause of the world's delay can't be ignored. Even as news circulated that Hitler had ordered the murder of Ernest Röhm and hundreds more, proclaiming himself Der Führer (grand leader) when President Paul von Hindenburg died that summer of 1934, almost no one resisted or even objected.

Why? The answer is worship. What kept world leaders at bay and fashioned a sterile environment for the incubation of insanity was the absolute adoration of Hitler by the majority of the German people.

The German masses worshiped Adolf Hitler with a loyalty and passion that shielded his rise from sustainable opposition. Women wept in the streets as his car passed by. Men dug up and saved a portion of sod on which Der Führer's foot had fallen.

If you're wondering why I'm writing about Hitler and the Nazis to open this week's study, it's because I want to make it clear that not all worship is good, and not all worship is vertical. Thankfully, we'll have an opportunity to strike a much more positive tone throughout the rest of the week as we explore the kind of unashamed adoration that brings God's glory down into the midst of a vertical church.

Day 1 /

WHY WORSHIP MATTERS

TODAY'S SCRIPTURE FOCUS >

"As soon as Solomon finished his prayer, fire came down from heaven and consumed the burnt offering and the sacrifices, and the glory of the LORD filled the temple. And the priests could not enter the house of the LORD, because the glory of the LORD filled the LORD's house. When all the people of Israel saw the fire come down and the glory of the LORD on the temple, they bowed down with their faces to the ground on the pavement and worshiped and gave thanks to the LORD, saying, 'For he is good, for his steadfast love endures forever.' " 2 Chronicles 7:1-3

I was sitting in my office at Arlington Heights Evangelical Free Church in August 1988 during my last day of employment there. My boxes were packed with books, and a tiny Macintosh computer from the fledgling Apple Company was on my desk. I had never published a single written word, but I sat down that afternoon and wrote what eventually became known as the four pillars of Harvest Bible Chapel:

- Unashamed adoration
- Unapologetic preaching
- Unafraid witness
- Unceasing prayer

By God's grace those pillars have become the foundation of our ministry both at Harvest and around the world. But back then I was 27, barely out of seminary, and simply trying to find a biblical answer to the most important question a pastor can ask: What does God bless?

So many people at that time—and really, throughout the history of the church—were flocking and floundering in the foolishness of asking, "What do people want in church?" But the Lord graced my novice mind with a more vertical question: What does God want in a church?

We're going to explore all four of those pillars throughout the remainder of this study, starting this week with unashamed adoration—a vertical understanding of worship.

What do you think of when you hear the word *worship*?

In your mind what are the components of an ideal worship experience?

THE MOST IMPORTANT THING WE DO

What's the root of all sin? I don't mean the worst sin or the one you struggle with most. But what specifically drives all of our acts of sin and rebellion against God?

How would you answer that question?

I've often heard people say pride is the root of all sin, but that's not correct. The right answer is idolatry, which is what happens when worship is directed to an unworthy person or object. Pride, the wrong view of self, often fuels idolatry, but the ultimate sin is placing anyone or anything on the throne that belongs to God alone.

That's the first message God delivered in His Ten Commandments: "You shall have no other gods before me" (Ex. 20:3). And that's the reality Jesus reinforced when He talked about the greatest commandment: "You shall love the Lord your God with all your heart and with all your soul and with all your mind" (Matt. 22:37).

Record how the following Scriptures contribute to your understanding of idolatry.

Isaiah 44:9-20

1 Corinthians 10:1-22

Galatians 4:8-11

Maybe you're wondering why idolatry is the root of all sin and why it's so destructive in our lives. The answer has to do with the extreme power of worship.

When Jesus said, "Where your treasure is, there your heart will be also" (Matt. 6:21), He was punctuating the absolute centrality of worship as the determinant for every human future. Indeed, worship or adoration is the most powerful expression a human being is capable of.

The highest and most powerful human experience is to express our love to the most worthy object of that affection; that's the core of what I'm trying to express with the concept of being vertical rather than horizontal. When we elevate Christ's worthiness, when we lift up His glory, we discover our greatest joy.

When have you had a powerful experience of worshiping God?

What emotions did you feel and what thoughts did you have that made this a vertical worship experience?

The greatest sin, then, is directing that adoration elsewhere, not only because it insults God but also because it insulates our hearts from the delight we were created to revel in. To fail at worship is the greatest failure a human is capable of, with the gravest and most immediate consequences.

WORSHIP BRINGS GOD HIMSELF

One reason vertical worship is so powerful is that it brings the manifest presence of God. As a reminder, God is omnipresent, which means He's everywhere. He inhabits all places and all things. But God's manifest presence is experiencing God here with us, moving and ministering in the church.

That's what we want in a vertical church and in a vertical relationship with God. We desire God's manifest presence in our lives and in the church, just as David wrote in Psalm 27:4:

> *One thing have I asked of the LORD,*
> *that will I seek after:*
> *that I may dwell in the house of the LORD*
> *all the days of my life,*
> *to gaze upon the beauty of the LORD*
> *and to inquire in his temple.*

Today's Scripture Focus gives us a picture of God showing up in a powerful way because of vertical worship. God had given King Solomon the opportunity to build a temple for His presence, which permanently replaced the tabernacle, or tent, where God's presence dwelled from the time of Moses until the time of David. When the construction of the temple was finished, Solomon kicked off a huge party for all Israel to worship and celebrate God. And when I say huge, I mean *huge*. In the middle of that celebration, Solomon offered a worshipful prayer to God on behalf of the community.

Read 2 Chronicles 5:11-14. What stands out to you about the worship celebration described in these verses?

Read the opening of Solomon's prayer in 2 Chronicles 6:12-17. How would you describe Solomon's attitude toward God?

In the midst of all that fervent worship and heartfelt prayer, God showed up:

> *As soon as Solomon finished his prayer, fire came down from heaven and consumed the burnt offering and the sacrifices, and the glory of the LORD filled the temple. And the priests could not enter the house of the LORD, because the glory of the LORD filled the LORD's house. When all the people of Israel saw the fire come down and the glory of the LORD on the temple, they bowed down with their faces to the ground on the pavement and worshiped and gave thanks to the LORD, saying, "For he is good, for his steadfast love endures forever."*
> 2 Chronicles 7:1-3

Would you like that kind of experience in your relationship with God? Would you like to see that kind of window-rattling, earth-shattering, life-changing moment in your church?

Record three words that describe your current experiences with worship.

How would you like your experiences with worship to change or improve in the future?

What steps can you take to make those changes or improvements happen?

If you want what Solomon experienced and what I've had the pleasure of experiencing as God's glory has come down in our church, concentrate this week on the power of vertical worship. Commit yourself to the adoration of Christ and His glory—and to nothing else.

Because when a believing community amplifies worship as their ultimate priority, they're shaped by that adoration into the most powerful human force possible.

WHAT IS WORSHIP?

TODAY'S SCRIPTURE FOCUS   >

"Ascribe to the Lord, O heavenly beings,

ascribe to the Lord glory and strength.

Ascribe to the Lord the glory due his name;

worship the Lord in the splendor of holiness." Psalm 29:1-2

By all indications from Scripture, John the Baptist was a pretty interesting guy. Not only did Isaiah prophesy about his appearance (see Isa. 40:3), but Matthew 3 also says, "John wore a garment of camel's hair and a leather belt around his waist, and his food was locusts and wild honey" (v. 4). That sounds like a guy who'd have some stories!

What I like most about John the Baptist is that he gave one of the most succinct and sincere expressions of a worshiper's heart that can be found in the New Testament:

> *A discussion arose between some of John's disciples and a Jew over purification.*
> *And they came to John and said to him, "Rabbi, he who was with you across*
> *the Jordan, to whom you bore witness—look, he is baptizing, and all are going*
> *to him." John answered, "A person cannot receive even one thing unless*
> *it is given him from heaven. You yourselves bear me witness, that I said,*
> *'I am not the Christ, but I have been sent before him.' The one who has*
> *the bride is the bridegroom. The friend of the bridegroom, who stands*
> *and hears him, rejoices greatly at the bridegroom's voice. Therefore this joy*
> *of mine is now complete. He must increase, but I must decrease."* John 3:25-30

What can we learn about John from these words?

What can we learn about Jesus?

"He must increase, but I must decrease" (v. 30). That's a vertical perspective on worship. Because when you worship, you're saying, "This one is worth more." At the same time, you're implying, "I am worth less." Worship is the magnification of God and the minimization of self.

Do you find it difficult or easy to minimize yourself and become less? Why?

What does it look like practically for people to minimize themselves in order to worship God?

DEFINITIONS

The Hebrew word translated *worship* in the Old Testament literally means *to fall or prostrate yourself before someone on the ground, touching your forehead to earth.* Both physically and figuratively, worship involves bowing or prostrating yourself before someone in humility; it's actually a picture of subservience.

For example, look at the way Moses responded to God's proclamation of His goodness and character on Mount Sinai: "Moses quickly bowed his head toward the earth and worshiped" (Ex. 34:8).

Read the following passages from the Old Testament and record how they contribute to your understanding of worship.

Deuteronomy 11:13-17

Joshua 5:13-15

Nehemiah 8:5-8

In the New Testament two words describe this action translated *worship.* One is the word *proskuneo,* which means *to kiss toward or to kiss the hand.* This word carries the idea of adoration. For example, John used the word *proskuneo* when writing about his vision of eternity:

> *Whenever the living creatures give glory and honor and thanks*
> *to him who is seated on the throne, who lives forever and ever,*
> *the twenty-four elders fall down before him who is seated on the*
> *throne and worship him who lives forever and ever.* Revelation 4:9-10

The elders worship God because they adore God.

The second word is *latreuo,* meaning *to give or to pay homage.* It's often translated *serve* in the New Testament. Talking about idolaters, Paul wrote, "They exchanged the truth about God for a lie and worshiped and served the creature rather than the Creator, who is blessed forever!" (Rom. 1:25).

How can our service to God express worship?

MORE THAN SINGING?

I often read or hear a servant of Christ insist that worship is more than singing. We're frequently told that making a meal for your family, cleaning your car, and helping your neighbor are all acts of worship. Well, I'm not so sure about that.

When these acts grow from our love for God and are done to demonstrate that love, I'd agree that they're worshipful, but technically, they aren't worship. I'm not trying to parse the meanings of words with undue rigor, but we need to be precise in our definitions if we want to accurately embrace the very purpose of our existence.

Worship is the actual act of ascribing worth directly to God. Worshipful actions may do this indirectly, but when the Bible commands and commends worship as our highest expression, it's specifically talking about a direct, intentional, vertical outpouring of adoration. Although that doesn't have to include music, it does have to be direct; it does have to rise above the worshipful and actually ascribe worth to God.

Remember that word *ascribe*. It's not a common term, but the idea of ascribing worth is a great way to think about worship. It means giving God what He deserves or giving Him credit for what He's done. That's what David was doing in Today's Scripture Focus:

> *Ascribe to the LORD, O heavenly beings,*
> *ascribe to the LORD glory and strength.*
> *Ascribe to the LORD the glory due his name;*
> *worship the LORD in the splendor of holiness.* Psalm 29:1-2

Worship is mind, emotions, and will engaged in whole-person ascription of worth.

Based on what you've read, how would you define *worship* in your own words?

According to your definition, what are some activities that can ascribe worth to God?

Nothing brings glory down in church as quickly and as powerfully as when God's people unashamedly adore God's great Son, Jesus Christ. That's not a few enthusiasts in the front row when the service starts; it's a room packed to the walls with fired-up Christians. I'm not talking about a testimony of someone's personal benefit that resulted from gospel belief; I'm talking about passionate ascription of worth to the God of the gospel. When that happens, an unbeliever coming into the service will "worship God and declare that God is really among you" (1 Cor. 14:25).

At the same time, any church activities that dilute, diminish, or detract from worship destroy verticality. They deny the priority of doxology and forfeit what vertical church is all about: God's glory.

What activities may be blocking your ability—corporately or individually—to worship God?

What can be done to better align those activities with a vertical focus?

WORSHIP THE SON

I want to reemphasize what I said earlier: "Nothing brings glory down in church as quickly and as powerfully as when God's people unashamedly adore *God's great Son, Jesus Christ.*" Those last five words are critical to a vertical understanding of worship: vertical worship is all about Jesus Christ.

Scripture says God freely gave His Son to demonstrate His love for us sinners. That incredible sacrifice, so counterintuitive to how father love works, is the engine that drives the Father's passion to see His Son elevated in our churches. The passion of God the Father is to see Jesus receive the honor due Him from the church He "obtained with His own blood" (Acts 20:28).

Scripture says it pleases the Father that all the fullness of the Godhead dwells in Jesus in bodily form (see Col. 1:19), that Christ is the radiance of the glory of God and the exact imprint of his nature" (Heb. 1:3), and that those who spurn the Son of God are worthy of greater punishment (see Heb. 10:26-31). So we shouldn't be surprised that God the Father shows up in power by the Holy Spirit when God the Son is unashamedly adored.

What are some ways you specifically worship Jesus Christ?

Are there moments in your life when you've felt unashamed adoration for Jesus? What did you experience in those moments?

What are some practices you could use to ascribe worth more fully to God's great Son both now and in the future?

Day 3 /

THE DANGERS OF DEFICIENT WORSHIP

TODAY'S SCRIPTURE FOCUS >

"The hour is coming, and is now here, when the true worshipers will worship the Father in spirit and truth, for the Father is seeking such people to worship him. God is spirit, and those who worship him must worship in spirit and truth." John 4:23-24

When pastors on our staff reach the landmark of having served a decade or more at Harvest, we honor them with a ring that represents both our thanks and our common convictions. Engraved on each ring is the second half of Today's Scripture Focus: "God is spirit, and those who worship him must worship in spirit and truth."

I don't think any verse has had a greater impact on the philosophy of ministry at our church than John 4:24. And I'll admit to liking the fact that Jesus spoke those words during one of His most outrageous conversations, when you consider the culture of His day.

Read John 4:1-29. What are the key images in these verses? What do they communicate?

What can we learn about worship from these verses?

What do you make of the disciples' reaction to Jesus' conversation in verse 27?

In John 4 the term *worship* is used 10 times in just five verses. A thirsty Jesus encountered a sinful woman who tried to change the subject from fornication to worship geography, but Jesus cut her off at the pass. From the lips of Christ during that conversation we learn four important elements of worship:

1. Worship is not a matter of where but who.
2. Worship must always be genuine, and God is seeking true worshipers.
3. Worship is not a matter of sincerity alone but also of truth.
4. Worship in truth alone is deficient unless it is also worship in spirit.

I want to focus on those last two elements today as we explore the dangers of deficient worship.

WHEN TRUTH IS MISSING

When we actively participate in worship without a proper understanding of the truth about God and His place in the universe, something bad happens. It's called idolatry.

Now I can already hear someone out there saying, "There are no golden calves or Asherah poles in my home or my sphere of influence, so I can't have a problem with idolatry." Are you sure? Because the simple definition of *idolatry* is *worship that's directed at anything other than God.*

Recently we surveyed a group of people at Harvest and asked them to name something Christians worship instead of God. Let's go through the top five responses together and see whether the Holy Spirit nudges you with conviction about these or any other areas of idolatry in your life.

5. We worship our families. I love my wife, I love my children, and I would die for any member of my family. But if I adore my family at the highest level—at the level where God is supposed to be adored—that's idolatry.

That kind of idolatry often shows through during difficult times. People say, "God is failing me because my marriage is on the rocks" or "God is failing me because my kids are sick or struggling." That's idolatry. The same is true for those who desperately want a spouse and/or children but don't have them yet. They say, "My life will never be full or complete until I get the family I want." That's idolatry too.

What do you like best about your family today?

Are you in any danger of worshiping or valuing your family more than God? Why or why not?

4. We worship our possessions. It's not wrong to have things, but it becomes wrong when things have you. And things *can* have you; nobody is immune from worshiping their possessions, and that's idolatry. Psalm 62:10 says, "If riches increase, set not your heart on them."

What possessions have *had* you in the past? What happened to them?

Are you in any danger of idolatry today when it comes to your possessions? Why or why not?

3. We worship famous people. Maybe it's a bad person. Maybe it's a good person. Maybe it's a Hollywood celebrity. Maybe it's a person in ministry, and you get all their books and listen to their teaching every day. But nothing good will ever happen when you put a human being in the place of God. That's idolatry. We're on this earth to worship Jesus Christ, who is the only One who never fails us.

List some people you admire most today.

Are you in any danger of putting those people in place of God? Why or why not?

2. We worship our careers. Thank God for our jobs. It's a privilege and a wonderful provision of God to have a career. But we must never worship our careers. We must never allow our identities to become so tied up with our jobs that they become the most important thing about us, because that's idolatry, and it will fall. God said, "My glory I give to no other" (Isa. 42:8), and He will tear anything down that gets in His place.

That goes for jobs in the marketplace, as well as for full-time ministry. I can't love ministry more than I love God. The Lord Himself has to be first, not my service for Him.

What do you like best about your job?

Are you in any danger of placing that job in God's appointed place? Why or why not?

1. We worship ourselves. Self-worship is the story of our culture. Many sources tell me every day that the primary road to happiness is for me to do whatever I want. To say whatever I want. To be whoever I want. To be with whomever I want. And whatever happens in life, the highest value is my personal happiness. That's idolatry.

Do you worship yourself? Explain your answer.

What are some other things Christians worship instead of God? What are some other possible areas of idolatry in your life?

All five of those things are good if kept in proper perspective, but all five can be extremely damaging sources of worship that is deficient in truth. Worship grounded in truth is worship of God alone.

WHEN THE SPIRIT IS MISSING

We're also in danger if our worship of God is entirely based on truth while being devoid of the spirit. And I'm talking about the human spirit here rather than the Holy Spirit.

The church in which I grew up specialized in what I now describe as shoulders-up worship. We sang lots of hymns, every verse packed with mostly outstanding theology. The problem was that the worship was mostly intellectual. Great theology raced by us at a pace so dizzying that the only impression we were left with was "That was all so true."

We affirmed truth, but there was little spirit in our worship. We understood what we sang, we believed it, and we sought to fix our eyes on it, but church was more like a recitation of the periodic table than a hand-over-heart, tearful rendition of the pledge of allegiance to our living God.

Is God satisfied with that? I always thought He was, and all of the people I knew agreed. But now I've come to realize the truth.

Here's what we're told in Deuteronomy 6:5, a central passage in the Old Testament: "You shall love the LORD your God with all your heart and with all your soul and with all your might." Jesus repeated that command in different forms several times in the Gospels (see Matt. 22:37; Mark 12:30; Luke 10:27).

The point is that we're to love God with our total being—with everything we have. That includes my mind, yes, but it also includes much more. My emotions. My will. My physical body. Everything.

Do you lean more toward shoulders-up worship or whole-being worship?

What steps can you take this week to more fully worship God in spirit and in truth?

This week and beyond, I pray you'll worship God in truth—in a way that recognizes His place both in the universe and in your own life. I also pray you'll worship God in spirit as you give your whole being to the kind of adoration that engages God and brings His glory down for all to see.

Day 4 /

FOUR LITTLE WORDS

TODAY'S SCRIPTURE FOCUS >

"Oh come, let us sing to the LORD;

let us make a joyful noise to the rock of our salvation!

Let us come into his presence with thanksgiving;

let us make a joyful noise to him with songs of praise!"

Psalm 95:1-2

Yesterday I mentioned that my church of origin specialized in shoulders-up worship, which meant I did too as I grew up. In fact, it wasn't until a trip to California as a Bible-college graduate that the Holy Spirit powerfully met me and tuned my heart to sing His praise both in truth *and* spirit. It happened when my aunt and uncle took me one Sunday to Calvary Chapel in Costa Mesa. At the time I had no idea I was entering a church just 10 years into the 20th century's greatest outpouring of conversions, church planting, and original worship. I'd heard Pastor Chuck Smith teach the Bible by radio, but I was unfamiliar with Calvary's fresh approach to worship.

That experience of worship shattered my previous assumptions of what church could be. Just a couple of guitar players sat on stools and led the worship, but their sweet simplicity set my biblical-worship bar at a whole new level. More than the platform talent, though, it was the worshipers around me looking up, raising their hands or kneeling, quietly singing with an expression that shouted sincerity. I'd never witnessed such Jesus joy, and it flooded every countenance of every face. It was the first time I remember raising my arms in worship or feeling my cheeks wet with tears of love for Christ. Purity and quiet passion flowed first into me and then out through me with a depth that felt physical.

What have you liked best about your recent experiences in worship?

Have you ever participated in a life-changing moment of worship? If so, what happened? If not, what do you hope to experience in the future?

If your heart can humbly admit your parched spiritual condition and the need to move beyond God information to God experience, what we're studying today can literally change your life. Specifically, four little words can elevate your worship experience above entertainment and beyond the mundane to bring down the glory of God.

VERTICAL

As I've reflected on that life-changing night, one detail stands out most and has made all the difference in my worship since: the people sang *to* the Lord, not *about* Him. That's not a revolutionary idea. The idea of singing to the Lord is mentioned several times in Scripture, including Today's Scripture Focus.

Do you regularly obey the Bible's call to "sing to the LORD" (Ps. 95:1) rather than about Him?

Take a moment to look at the lyrics of your favorite songs and hymns. How many of them are horizontal, singing about God, and how many are vertical, singing to Him?

My concern with the indirect language of horizontal songs is that it betrays the mistaken notion that God is not present with us as we worship, especially in His church. When you or I stand in a circle speaking about someone who suddenly enters the room, we intuitively stop talking about the person, or we immediately welcome the person into the center of what we're saying. We'd never continue talking about the person when we know he or she can hear us.

In the same way, if we believe God is present in our worship as He promises (see Ps. 22:3), we must direct all language of worship to Him and not merely about Him. Otherwise, our worship effectively ignores and potentially offends Him by talking about Him as thought He weren't present.

See if you can think of three hymns or songs that are written to God in a vertical way. (Two examples are "Holy, Holy, Holy" and "Joyful, Joyful, We Adore Thee.")

SIMPLE

A second characteristic of worship at Calvary Chapel was the simplicity of what we sang. The melodies were simple. The words were easy to grasp and remember.

If that sounds beneath you, I recommend changing your mind-set. Because, with all due respect to hymns filled with great theology, that level of complexity is not what Scripture reveals as God's personal preference for our worship. Yes, God has worship preferences, and becoming vertical in our adoration is all about understanding those prerogatives and shaping our actions to fit them.

Read the following passages of Scripture and record what you observe about the patterns of worship in heaven.

Isaiah 6:1-3

Revelation 4:6-11

Revelation 5:11-14

Do you prefer simple or complex songs in your times of worship? Why?

Worship that God delights to receive should pattern itself after the sincere simplicity for which He has revealed a preference. Worship that brings glory down respects and must reflect biblical theology, but it should be more like loving, personal communication and less like an ordination statement.

EMOTIVE

I've heard a good bit of criticism of contemporary worship through the years, and much of it centers on repetition. "Why do we have to keep singing the same words over and over?" asks the shoulders-up worshiper I used to be.

When I hear those criticisms, I again recommend that people look to the Bible. Psalm 119 has more than 175 different references to the Word of God, for example. Psalm 136 has 26 repetitions of the phrase "His love endures forever." See, it's actually the absence of repetition that keeps our minds racing across the theological peaks of most great hymns and blocks our emotions from entering our worship experience.

Reviewing, meditating, reflecting, and pondering are important biblical concepts in worship, and they're assisted by repetition. That's because each trip over the same terrain allows God to "enlarge my heart" (Ps. 119:32).

Do you enjoy repetition in worship? Why or why not? What are the advantages of continually returning to the same concepts and phrases?

Simple repetition, however, isn't enough. We need genuine emotion in our worship. Indeed, the idea of worship without emotion in our engagement with God should be as repulsive to us as any passionless interaction in a precious human relationship. My wife doesn't want to hear me recite a mere formula as an expression of scheduled affection for her. And God doesn't visit a shoulders-up, heartless recitation of "It's Sunday morning at 11:00, time to review the God formula." Relationship inevitably fails at the point of formula and flourishes when the whole person becomes fully engaged.

Do you truly *feel* something significant during your expressions of adoration to God?

Who receives your most passionate expressions of love during a given week? What does your answer say about your relationship with and worship of God?

PHYSICAL

The biblical injunction to whole-person worship includes the command to "love the Lord your God … with all your strength" (Mark 12:30). That can mean strength of passion or strength of intellect, but it shouldn't exclude the most obvious understanding of strength—not as an adjective describing the other capacities to love but as a category by itself.

The idea of a spiritual act like worship being physical may seem strange to you at first, but it's both biblical and beneficial. Involving your body in worship aids in joining emotion with intellect. Indeed, King David, the greatest worshiper the world has ever known, exemplified physicality in worship.

As you read the following passages of Scripture, record which body parts are referenced and how they can aid us in physically worshiping God.

Psalm 116:1   **Psalm 47:1; 63:4**

Psalm 123:1   **Psalm 95:6**

Psalm 3:3

Keep in mind that these physical expressions of whole-being worship aren't like optional items you might check when ordering a sandwich. Because they're commanded and modeled in Scripture, we need to employ them increasingly, without using personality or tradition as an excuse.

Are you willing to incorporate physical acts and expressions into your worship? Why or why not?

Through the years I've come to accept that God has a far greater capacity to receive varied worship expressions than we have for them to exist together in one church. So I'm not saying all churches should look, feel, or sound the same. What matters is that we not allow our culture or other excuses to place a cap on the fullest expression we can humanly offer to God—for He is surely worthy.

Day 5 /

EXPERIENCING VERTICAL WORSHIP

TODAY'S SCRIPTURE FOCUS >

"Enter his gates with thanksgiving,

and his courts with praise!

Give thanks to him; bless his name!" Psalm 100:4

I don't know about you, but I usually don't include interior design among God's many attributes. Perhaps I should, because there's no denying the weighty and specific attention God gave to Moses and the Israelites about the construction of the tabernacle. In fact, God told Moses, "Exactly as I show you concerning the pattern of the tabernacle, and of all its furniture, so you shall make it" (Ex. 25:9).

Read Exodus 26:1-25. What stands out to you most about God's instructions for building the tabernacle?

What images did you find interesting or unusual? Why?

Today I want us to explore together God's specific intentions for designing the tabernacle the way He did. My goal isn't a thorough exegesis of the finer points of tabernacle furnishings, although every piece of equipment God requested had special significance. Rather, I want to show the progression God designed for His people to follow during times of worship.

The tabernacle and later the temple were the central places of worship for the Israelites, and God deliberately created five spaces in which they participated in worship experiences: an ascent, a gate, a courtyard, the holy place, and the holy of holies (also called the most holy place). For many years people in vertical churches have found great profit in building their worship services around the progression of adoration reflected in these successive spaces.

Record what you already know about each of the five spaces in the Old Testament tabernacle.

As we study an order of worship that mirrors God's design for His people, you will learn postures and attitudes that will help you make the most of any worship experience.

WORSHIP AS WE ARRIVE

When the ancient Israelites traveled to Jerusalem for various festivals and celebrations, they sang a specific group of songs as they journeyed up Mount Zion toward Jerusalem. These psalms of ascent are recorded as Psalms 120–134.

These psalms make it clear that the people started worshiping even before they reached God's house. Each psalm intentionally directed the singers' gaze vertically, asking participants to lift up their eyes, look to the hills, and worship the Maker of heaven and earth.

Read the following psalms and record how they contribute to a vertical focus.

Psalm 121:1-8

Psalm 125:1-5

Psalm 131:1-3

How could those psalms help prepare your heart for worship?

Worshipers in ancient Israel couldn't be expected to voluntarily or automatically shed the patterns of thinking that prohibit full engagement with God just because they arrived at the tabernacle. The same is true of people who arrive at churches today.

That's why vertical churches include a call to worship each week. This call can be an echo of the psalms of ascent, a direct Scripture reading, or an invitation for God's manifest presence. We don't assume everyone who enters our worship center is ready to offer praise and adoration to God. So the call to worship is the part of our service plan that elicits engagement at the fullest level from worshipers.

Similarly, when you prepare to enter a worship service, it's necessary for you to prepare your heart. Work with the Holy Spirit to let go of the stresses, burdens, and irritations that can block a life-changing encounter with God's manifest presence and glory.

How do you prepare yourself to participate in a worshipful experience?

What practical steps could you take to prepare yourself better?

WORSHIP AT THE GATE

Each of us knows the joy of reaching a destination after an arduous journey and entering the place we envisioned during our travel. That's what the Israelites experienced after journeying miles and miles to reach the tabernacle. And that's what we should experience as we enter worship. Excitement should peak as we begin to engage with the One in whose honor we've gathered.

Thanksgiving is the proper response in these moments, as the psalmist declared:

> *Enter his gates with thanksgiving,*
> *and his courts with praise!*
> *Give thanks to him; bless his name!* Psalm 100:4

And again in Psalm 118:

> *Open to me the gates of righteousness,*
> *that I may enter through them*
> *and give thanks to the LORD.* Psalm 118:19

Vertical churches follow the call to worship with several upbeat, celebratory elements—both Scripture and song—that express our gratitude to God. In the same way, you can train your mind to respond with thanksgiving when you enter a time of worship and begin to enjoy a vertical encounter with Him.

What are you most thankful for right now? Why?

Speaking practically, how can you train yourself to begin a worship experience with thanksgiving and gratitude?

THE COURTS OF TESTIMONY

Thinking back to ancient Israel, I picture the courts of the tabernacle as a gathering place. I see the worshipers coming together in community, then looking as a single group toward the holy place and the place of God's presence at the interior of the tabernacle.

In a similar way, we arrive at church today as individuals or families, only to discover afresh as we begin to worship that we are in truth part of the larger family of God. Together in Christian community we have the incredible opportunity to testify to one another from our current experiences about God's great faithfulness.

Vertical churches use this third segment of worship to focus on that theme: testimony. Our songs are testimony songs that speak about God's great works among us; think of "Lord, I Lift Your Name on High," for example. We also frequently take a break from singing during this time and focus on an element of church life. That could be a live testimony, a powerful story told through video, or worshipers lining up at microphones to read Scriptures that have proved true in recent experiences.

As you worship God, be sure you emphasize this element of testimony as well. After you've expressed thanksgiving and gratitude for His presence, remind yourself of what God has done for you, in you, and through you. Speak with Him about what's dragging you down and lifting you up.

How can you include this element of testimony in your corporate worship experiences?

How can you include it in your private worship?

THE PLACE OF PREPARATION

The holy place was the private area where the priests prepared the sin offerings to be taken into the holy of holies. It had several significant pieces of furniture that focused on God's faithfulness to His people and prefigured the glorious truths of the gospel. Further, it was here that the priest washed, dressed, and readied himself for the holy of holies, where the ark of the covenant waited.

In a vertical church, after the focus on testimony, the content of what we sing and say again turns vertical. The songs are noticeably more about exalting God Himself and laying hold of His sufficiency. Just as the priest had to follow carefully prescribed preparations before going behind the curtain, we must make sure we have wrapped ourselves afresh in the robe of Christ's righteousness before we encounter His presence.

As you participate in worship, an attitude of repentance and cleansing appropriately expresses your holy fear of going any further into God's manifest presence unprepared. Confess your sin. Confess your unworthiness. Ask God to make you clean.

Read Isaiah 6:1-7. When have you felt the depth of your sinfulness in comparison to God's glory?

What steps can you take in worship to be cleansed and prepared to experience God?

THE PLACE OF HOLY PRESENCE

In holy-of-holies worship we experience what the hymn writer described as "lost in wonder, love and praise."[1] Here there's not a syllable of testimony or even a small scrap of "what God has done for me." No one is clapping anymore as joyful exuberance is eclipsed by the awesome presence of Almighty God Himself.

As you participate in this phase of worship, entering the presence of God Himself, let go of everything else. There should be nothing about you and everything about God. Stop thinking about God's actions on your behalf. Instead, concentrate on His exalted splendor and surpassing beauty. Seek no benefit from this time other than the joy of being lost in the satisfaction you were created to long for.

This is the fulfillment that can be found only when God is rightly adored in whole-person worship by the entire congregation and when His glory comes down.

What's your reaction to this description of worship? Why?

Are you willing to let go of yourself to fully experience God's presence? What would that look like for you?

To encounter God in that way is to be gladly small—reduced to the reality of my minute existence and relieved to admit the truth about myself in the presence of true glory. May it be so for you this week and for the rest of your life.

How will you approach personal and corporate worship differently next time as a result of this week's study?

1. Charles Wesley, "Love Divine, All Loves Excelling," *Baptist Hymnal* (Nashville: LifeWay Worship, 2008), 172.

WHAT BRINGS THE GLORY DOWN

UNAPOLOGETIC PREACHING

WEEK SIX

START

Welcome back to this small-group discussion of *Vertical Church*.

The application challenge from the previous session involved replacing one of your daily activities with a time of worship. If you're comfortable, relate your experiences worshiping God this week.

What did you like best from week 5 in the workbook? What questions do you still have?

How do you react to this statement? "The highest and most powerful human experience is to express our love to the most worthy object of that affection."

How do you hope to grow in the short term as a worshiper of Jesus Christ? How do you hope to grow in the long term?

To prepare to view the DVD segment, read these verses aloud.

The word of the cross is folly to those who are perishing, but to us who are being saved it is the power of God. For it is written,

*"I will destroy the wisdom of the wise,
and the discernment of the discerning I will thwart."*

Where is the one who is wise? Where is the scribe? Where is the debater of this age? Has not God made foolish the wisdom of the world? For since, in the wisdom of God, the world did not know God through wisdom, it pleased God through the folly of what we preach to save those who believe. For Jews demand signs and Greeks seek wisdom, but we preach Christ crucified, a stumbling block to Jews and folly to Gentiles, but to those who are called, both Jews and Greeks, Christ the power of God and the wisdom of God.
1 Corinthians 1:18-24

WATCH

Complete the viewer guide below as you watch DVD session 6.

What is _____?

Preach means to _____, to announce, to publicly proclaim.

Whom do we _____?

A THREE-PART TESTIMONY

1. The testimony of _____
2. _____ _____
3. Him _____

In every message: Christ our _____, the gospel.
In every message: Christ our _____.

Christianity is not a faith of _____ _____. It is a faith of _____ _____.

Why do we _____?

It's things that have changed that _____ not and _____ not have changed.
Those are the real issues.

God has ordained the method of preaching because it's the method that keeps His messengers
_____.

How do we _____?

Say what the _____ says.

What happens when we _____?

Preach the authority of God's Word without _____.

When the man of God in the fear of God takes the Word of God and proclaims the heart of God,
that is the _____ of God coming down.

WHAT YOU CAN DO

1. _____ the Word of God.
2. _____ the Word of God.
3. _____ the Word of God.
4. _____ the Word of God.

RESPOND

Discuss the DVD segment with your group, using the questions below.

> What did you like best about the DVD segment? Why?

> What emotions do you experience when you hear the word *preach*? Why?

> Who are some of your favorite preachers? What do you like best about their preaching?

> How have you been impacted by the ministry of preaching in local churches?

> How do you react to this statement? "All preaching is the testimony of God—the story. But all preaching, more specifically, is the Word of God, yes, and then the gospel of the Son of God is the bull's-eye. Scope that in. All preaching needs to be that."

> What are the differences between proclamation and discussion in a local church? What are the advantages of each experience?

> When we attend a sermon, what steps can we take to make the most of that experience as individuals? How can we make the most of that experience corporately?

APPLICATION

Spend time in your pastor's shoes this week by preparing a sermon of your own. It doesn't have to be long or profound, but identify a topic, research, write an outline, and practice proclaiming "Jesus Christ and him crucified" (1 Cor. 2:2).

SCRIPTURE MEMORY FOR THIS WEEK
*All Scripture is breathed out by God and profitable for teaching,
for reproof, for correction, and for training in righteousness, that
the man of God may be competent, equipped for every good work.*
2 Timothy 3:16-17

READ WEEK 6 AND COMPLETE THE ACTIVITIES BEFORE THE NEXT GROUP EXPERIENCE.

WEEK 6

"All Scripture is breathed out by God and profitable for teaching, for reproof, for correction, and for training in righteousness, that the man of God may be competent, equipped for every good work."

2 Timothy 3:16-17

SAY IT IN A SENTENCE >

Preaching the authority of God's Word without apology, in the power of the Holy Spirit, brings glory down in a church.

REFLECTIONS OF A PREACHER >

In the early days at Harvest Bible Chapel, I was a tortured preacher. Sunday and Monday I roasted myself as I reviewed the ways my sermon had failed to arrest the hearts and minds of the people with biblical truth. On Tuesday, when I called first-time visitors and too frequently heard them waffle on their intent to return, I assumed I had overdone the passion, underdone the clarity, or missed the soul altogether. Wednesday I allowed myself to hope I could do better the next weekend and began in earnest to study the passage at hand. My excitement grew on Thursday as I discovered truth and planned a way to get it across effectively. On Friday I locked myself away, completing the outline for the bulletin and my notes for the pulpit in a 10-plus-hour marathon that reminded me of exam week in college. Saturday I spent with family, but as evening came, Kathy claims I would glaze over at some point and trade attentive listening for distant stares and what she came to affectionately call my Sermon Never-Never Land.

Here's what I've learned: biblical preaching demands effort, drains energy, and distracts attention from other things that also matter but demand less. Real preaching requires any offense to be resolved, sin to be surrendered, and distraction to be diminished. It's easy to do poorly and terrifically difficult to do well once—let alone week after week.

For almost 30 years preaching has been the crucible for my sanctification—the method God has used more than any other to shape my soul. I hope it has helped others; I know it's transformed me, and it's continued to do so through this very day.

If you're a preacher, you'll benefit from the vertical approach to proclamation outlined in this week's material. If you don't preach, you're not off the hook. Because whenever you attend a church service or hear a sermon, you're a participant in the preaching process. More important, your personal devotions should follow the same vertical path any good preacher takes to hear, accept, appreciate, and apply God's Word.

Day 1 /

THE ROLE OF PREACHING

TODAY'S SCRIPTURE FOCUS >

"I, when I came to you, brothers, did not come proclaiming to you the testimony of God with lofty speech or wisdom. For I decided to know nothing among you except Jesus Christ and him crucified." 1 Corinthians 2:1-2

Preaching is an up-and-down concept in today's culture. A lot of people consider it boring or a waste of time, and our cultural lexicon holds a negative connotation for *preaching* as a term. We say, "Don't be so preachy," for example, or "Don't preach at me about how I live my life."

At the same time, millions of men around the world dedicate themselves weekly to the practice of preaching God's Word. And literally hundreds of millions of people go to church every weekend to hear, grapple with, and apply the sermons.

No matter what your opinion is about preaching, this can't be denied: the faithful proclamation of God's Word has been and continues to be one of the most powerful forces in history for shaping cultures and the lives of individuals.

What words or images come to mind when you hear the word *preach*? What emotions do you experience?

How do you approach the preaching experience each week in your church? What do you hope happens during that experience?

As I wrote down the four pillars of a vertical church more than 25 years ago, verses like Today's Scripture Focus gave rise to the pillar that became my lifelong commitment: preaching the authority of God's Word without apology. And probably the single greatest shortcoming in the church today is the spectacle of pastors who sit in their offices with their Bibles closed, working on talks for people who want horizontal intuition instead of vertical inspiration.

In your opinion, what responsibilities does a preacher have during the week and during the sermon itself?

What responsibilities do members of the congregation have during and after the sermon?

As with all things vertical, the ultimate question about preaching and its role in God's design for His church has much less to do with what we expect or desire and much more to do with what God wants. We can better understand our role as preachers and church members if we have a clearer picture of what God had in mind with this challenging responsibility called preaching.

WHAT IS PREACHING?

Let's start our discussion on preaching with a few definitions and vocabulary words. While we often read about Jesus teaching in the New Testament, the gospel He left behind was always meant to be preached or proclaimed rather than taught in the same way we teach math or comma usage in school.

There are two primary Greek words translated *preach* or *preaching* in the New Testament. The first is *kēryssō*, which described a person of the royal court commissioned by the ruler to proclaim a message with a strong, resonant voice. Classical Greek literature emphasizes the herald himself, but biblical texts emphasize not the proclaimer but the manner and content of the proclamation itself. *Kēryssō* stresses a message of gravity and authority—something that must be listened to and obeyed.[1] In New Testament usage the true preacher is Christ Himself, so the herald must recognize his place as only a mouthpiece.[2]

The second word frequently translated as *preach* or *proclaim* in the English Bible is *euangelizo*. It's used 54 times in the New Testament, and while it still carries the idea of heralding, the message of the gospel is explicit in the word rather than implicit in the context, as with *kēryssō*.

With both terms the proclamation of God's message is of paramount importance, and the messenger is concerned only with the faithful transmission of the message so that the intended audience hears it. In other words, when we see the terms *preach* and *proclaim* in our English Bibles, they aren't exalting human preachers; they're telling us about the act of preaching itself. Preaching is much less about the person or the place it happens and more a pattern for the way God wants His message delivered.

As you read the following passages of Scripture, identify the person doing the preaching and the message being proclaimed.

Matthew 10:5-7

Mark 16:14-18

Acts 10:34-43

Ephesians 3:7-12

What do these verses communicate about the kinds of people called to preach? What do they communicate about the kinds of people to be preached to?

Here's my definition of *preaching*: *heralding, announcing, or publicly proclaiming a message of importance*. Now some believers certainly receive a special gift of preaching and/or teaching in the church. But anyone who receives the Word of truth has a responsibility to be a herald of that message.

That includes me, and it includes you too.

What does it mean to be a herald of God's Word in our everyday lives?

Speaking practically, how do we go about that kind of heralding throughout the week?

WHAT DO WE PREACH?

If *preaching* is defined as *heralding, announcing, or publicly proclaiming a message*, the next logical question is this: What message are we supposed to herald, announce, or proclaim as followers of Jesus? In other words, what are we supposed to preach?

First, we need to preach the Word of God. That message is clear in 2 Timothy 3:16-17:

> ***All Scripture is breathed out by God and profitable for teaching, for reproof, for correction, and for training in righteousness, that the man of God may be competent, equipped for every good work.***

All Scripture is inspired, or "breathed out by God." That means there's no excuse for a pastor to deliver points of human persuasion while the Bible—the absolute authority that incinerates human folly and "[fills] the hungry with good things" (Luke 1:53)—gathers dust on the corner of his desk. A pastor is called not to whip up the crowd with relevant pep talks, but to sound forth the Word of life.

God has given us His very breath in writing—always true, ever new, and eternally compelling when dispensed in His strength and with His authority. Therefore, to stand in a pulpit with a false authority flowing from the speaker's opinions and ideas is the height of presumption. Preaching with the authority of God's Word is the God-breathed, Scripture-saturated proclamation of eternal truth.

Nothing less will satisfy the preacher or members in a vertical church.

What place does the Bible have in your church's weekly worship services?

What place does God's Word have in your life during the week?

When Paul wrote his first letter to the Corinthians, he was writing to a local church infested with carnal, worldly, sexually immoral, materialistic, and divisive tendencies. Sound familiar? This morass of sin was consuming the church.

Having visited the Corinthians earlier, Paul reminded them in Today's Scripture Focus of the message he came to proclaim: "I, when I came to you, brothers, did not come proclaiming to you the testimony of God with lofty speech or wisdom" (1 Cor. 2:1).

That phrase "lofty speech" literally means *excellence of words*. The word translated "wisdom" comes from the Greek term *sophia*. In Greek culture wisdom had become something esoteric—a superior and inside knowledge. The Greek intellectuals highly valued a polished speaker who could stand up and wax eloquent. Indeed, what's translated as "lofty speech" could even be called pompous talk.

Sadly, some of today's preachers would fit well in that society. They make you think, *That guy sure likes the sound of his own voice. Why can't he talk like a regular person?* Paul didn't come across that way.

Look at how Paul continued in 1 Corinthians 2:2: "I decided to know nothing among you except Jesus Christ and him crucified." Wow!

Paul had three goals for his preaching. First was to make known the testimony of God (1 Cor. 2:1). Second, Paul wanted to proclaim Jesus Christ, the culmination of all God has done for us. And third, Paul hit the bull's-eye by preaching "him crucified." The death, burial, and resurrection of Jesus Christ was a primary the message of Paul's preaching. And it needs to be the focus of all preaching today.

What role did preaching play in introducing you to Jesus?

What role has preaching played in your continued connection to and service for Jesus?

What steps can you take this week to assist and enhance the proclamation of God's Word in your church?

One last thing. I know preachers who consider themselves inferior communicators, and it bothers them. I also know that many people bounce from one church to another because their current pastor isn't entertaining enough. Maybe they don't say that out loud, but it's a factor. And it's a shame.

Read 1 Corinthians 2:1-5. How did Paul characterize his proclamation?

Which are you more used to seeing in church: "plausible words of wisdom" or "demonstration of the Spirit and of power" (v. 5)?

Yes, public speaking is a skill. Those who are called to preach the Word of God should work on honing that skill to the best of their ability. But at the end of the day, a preacher's nothing more than a mouthpiece. We proclaim the Word of God. We preach Jesus Christ and Him crucified. That's what matters.

Day 2 /

LISTENING TO THE WORD

TODAY'S SCRIPTURE FOCUS   >

"The word of God is living and active, sharper than any two-edged sword, piercing to the division of soul and of spirit, of joints and of marrow, and discerning the thoughts and intentions of the heart. And no creature is hidden from his sight, but all are naked and exposed to the eyes of him to whom we must give account." Hebrews 4:12-13

What are some of the most valuable possessions in your home? I'm not talking about the people who live there. I'm talking about your stuff.

Record your most expensive possession and your possession with the most sentimental value.

Did your Bible make the list? I know; your Bible didn't cost nearly as much as your TV or your record collection. And in terms of sentimental value, you could run down to any Christian bookstore and get a replacement just about any day of the week. Even so, take a moment to think about what it means to have the Word of God on your bookshelf—to hold it in your hands. It's incredible!

This week we're focused on preaching God's Word. Not every Christian is called to be a vocational preacher, but every Christian is called to listen to the Word of God and proclaim it in their sphere of influence. The Word is the center of a believer's life; it's incredibly important and incredibly valuable. Therefore, listening to it and obeying it are the duty and delight of both preachers and congregations.

LIVING AND ACTIVE

Look, I'm a realist when it comes to church. I understand that some preaching is difficult to wade through. I've heard sermons that were nothing more than profitless Bible babbling that inflicted boredom on all who heard them. I'm sure you have too. That should never be the case.

What circumstances cause you to feel bored or frustrated during a preaching experience? What circumstances cause you to feel engaged and excited during preaching?

In college a veteran preacher named Trevor Baird taught me that "the greatest sin in the ministry is to bore people with the Bible," and I've gladly exhausted myself attempting never to do so. I've failed at times, but I've never done so with resignation or rationalization that the hearers were the problem.

The reason preaching should never be boring goes way beyond those of us who preach. It's because of the absolute wonder and majesty of what we preach: God's Word! That's what Today's Scripture Focus is all about:

> *The word of God is living and active, sharper than any two-edged sword, piercing to the division of soul and of spirit, of joints and of marrow, and discerning the thoughts and intentions of the heart. And no creature is hidden from his sight, but all are naked and exposed to the eyes of him to whom we must give account.* Hebrews 4:12-13

In what way are the words of the Bible similar to a sword?

When has God's Word revealed something that changed your attitudes or values?

Listening to the Word of God involves watchful and willing consideration of the text. When a pastor listens to God's Word, he places himself on God's operating table and invites Him to use His scalpel on his life. All of his thoughts and all of his actions stand uncovered and exposed.

The same is true for members of the congregation as they read the Word throughout the week and during the weekend sermon: the process begins at home and carries over to gathering with other believers at church. Indeed, listening to the Word of God is the key practice that keeps home and church seamlessly connected.

In what ways do you place yourself under the scrutiny of God's Word?

In what ways are you teaching your family to listen to God's Word?

Read Deuteronomy 6:4-9. What four examples are given of listening to God's Word at home?

Which of these could become a greater priority in your family life?

EXAMINING THE SCRIPTURES

When Paul entered Macedonia on his second missionary journey, he met acceptance, resistance, and rejection from the diverse population. He usually followed a set plan when he entered a city, starting his preaching ministry among the Jews and then branching out to teach the Gentiles as well.

We can learn a lot from Paul's methods and style of preaching, of course, but just as fascinating is the reaction of those who heard his message. Indeed, the contrast between his experiences in Thessalonica and Berea is striking.

Read Acts 17:1-9. How did the Thessalonians respond to Paul's preaching?

Read Acts 17:10-13. How did the Bereans respond to Paul's preaching?

As participants in preaching experiences and as students of God's Word throughout the week, we must never be satisfied by passively listening to the messages of preachers and other teachers. It's never to our benefit for us to say, "Pastor said it, so I believe it." No. Be like the Bereans and examine the concepts you hear proclaimed. Examine the insights you make while studying the Scriptures. Be an active listener to God's Word, not a passive hearer of horizontal claims.

After you listen to a sermon each weekend, what steps can you take to begin "examining the Scriptures daily to see if these things were so" (v. 11)?

One way we can follow the Berean example at church today is to hold an open Bible in our hands as we listen to the Word being preached. Sometimes I think easy access to the Bible has made many of us lax in our handling of the Scriptures. Some believers have even stopped bringing their Bibles to church. Would you show up to a tee time with Sergio Garcia and not bring your clubs? Would you go into battle without a weapon? Neither should you show up for an encounter with the awesome God of the universe without bringing your copy of His Word.

WHAT ARE YOU LISTENING FOR?

As I've said, those of us who proclaim God's Word should never be satisfied with casual or occasional references to the Scriptures. Preaching God's Word inevitably involves specific, encouraging, and sometimes painful application of the truth to life. As we examine the words of the Bible, therefore, we must pay careful attention to stories, verses, or single words that have a direct connection to our hearts.

In other words, if you want opportunities to apply God's Word as you read it or hear it preached, you must actively listen for those truths that can be and need to be applied in your life. Eugene Peterson wrote about this:

> Obedience is the thing, living in active response to the living God.
> The most important question we ask of this text is not, "What does
> this mean?" but "What can I obey?" A simple act of obedience
> will open up our lives to this text far more quickly than any
> number of Bible studies and dictionaries and concordances.[3]

Obedience should be our attitude as we open God's Word, as we study God's Word, and as we close God's Word.

How do you identify truths from God's Word that need to be obeyed?

What steps can you take to become more active in your efforts to apply God's Word?

In addition to listening for application opportunities, we need to listen for the story of Jesus. Biblical preaching begins and ends with Christ, and it doesn't stray far from Him in the middle. That's because biblical preaching centers on the gospel.

Just as you should expect to hear the gospel of Christ at the heart of biblical preaching, the same is true for your personal Bible study. All Scripture points toward and centers on the redemptive message of Jesus Christ. Therefore, God's Word has the authority to tell lost people how they can be saved and to tell Christians how they should live as disciples of Jesus.

Read the following passages and record ways they point to the life and work of Jesus.

Genesis 3:8-15

Psalm 19:7-14

Acts 9:36-43

Listen to the Word of God this week. Whenever you preach, hear a sermon, and personally study the Bible, actively focus your attention on the living, life-changing messages found only in God's Word.

ACCEPTING THE WORD OF GOD

TODAY'S SCRIPTURE FOCUS   >

"All Scripture is breathed out by God and profitable for teaching, for reproof, for correction, and for training in righteousness, that the man of God may be competent, equipped for every good work." 2 Timothy 3:16-17

There are a lot of people who don't go to the doctor, and those people cite a lot of different reasons as to why they don't go. Sometimes those reasons are financial. Other times they're practical; a person can't take time off work for an appointment, for instance.

But I'm convinced that most people who refuse to see a doctor do so because they simply don't want to hear bad news. And I don't think it's even the really bad news that scares them—cancer or spinal meningitis or that kind of thing. Rather, I believe there's a large segment of people in today's culture who don't want to be told their lifestyle is causing damage but could be fixed with discipline and healthy behavior.

GOD'S WORD IS PROFITABLE

This desire to avoid changes in lifestyle is also a reason more and more people choose not to attend church. We don't want to be told that our public vices and secret sins are causing spiritual damage that will impact eternity for us. We just want to keep doing what we've been doing. That's sad.

But what's really sad is the fact that many preachers in North America today aren't willing to proclaim a word of challenge or a message of correction; in other words, they don't want to deliver any bad news. They hope people will get the point without having to point it out to them.

There's a big problem with that approach, and it has to do with God's Word—where it comes from and how it operates in our lives.

Today's Scripture Focus begins with these words: "All Scripture is breathed out by God and profitable" (2 Tim. 3:16). That word translated *profitable* carries an intense sense of purpose: God's Word is intended to accomplish something and is effective at accomplishing it.

But profitable for what? The rest of Today's Scripture Focus lists four things:

1. Teaching. That's doctrine. Scripture teaches us what to believe.
2. Reproof. A reproof is when someone says, "Knock it off!" I love when I come to church and get a reproof, because one way I'm sure God loves me is when He says, "Cut that out." That's one of the things love says.
3. Correction. The idea of correction runs along the lines of "Do this, not that; here's the way to go now." It clarifies a mistake and points us in the right direction.
4. Training in righteousness. God's Word tells us how to do life in a way that avoids constant reproof and correction. Giving attention to what it says is profitable for us, including the hard stuff. When God says, "Don't," He means, "Don't hurt yourself!"

Read the following passages of Scripture and identify each one as teaching, reproof, correction, or training in righteousness.

James 1:2-4

James 1:5

James 1:17

James 4:13-15

Look again at Today's Scripture Focus. In recent months how has God's Word been profitable in your life?

Do you benefit from God's Word most often through biblical preaching or your personal study of the text? Explain your answer.

As human beings, we'll always need God's Word this side of eternity because we always require teaching, reproof, correction, and training in righteousness. We mostly experience this as individuals seeking to apply the truth of God in our lives, but 2 Timothy 3:16 is also corrective word for churches. Sometimes entire congregations require a new word and/or a change of direction.

For all of those reasons, one of the best ways you can pray for your pastor is to ask God to give him courage to preach the whole counsel of God. Also pray that God would bless your church—individually and corporately—with a willingness to listen and respond in obedience.

What practical steps can you take to be more faithful in praying for your pastor and the other members of your congregation?

What steps can you take to consciously approach preaching experiences and personal Bible study with a willingness to accept teaching, reproof, correction, and training in righteousness?

OPENNESS TO THE WORD

It's one thing for us to recognize when God uses His Word to teach, reprove, correct, and train us in righteousness; becoming aware of what God is doing is an important step. But other steps need to be taken as well.

For example, once we recognize what God's Word has to say, we need to actively accept that each instance of teaching, reproof, correction, and training actually comes from God. It was spoken directly and specifically to us. I'm not quibbling over semantics here. Before we can apply the truths of Scripture to our lives, we need to get straight in our mind that those truths have their source in God Himself—that they carry His authority.

When have you received advice from a person you didn't respect? What happened?

Whom do you respect most in life? How have you been impacted by their teaching, reproof, correction, and training?

Yesterday we looked at the contrasting responses to the gospel by the Bereans and the Thessalonians. Paul commended the Bereans because they examined his teaching to make sure it lined up with the truths of Scripture. Later, when Paul wrote to the church in Thessalonica, he complimented the believers there on the way they demonstrated a lasting acceptance of God's Word:

> *We also thank God constantly for this, that when you received the word of God, which you heard from us, you accepted it not as the word of men but as what it really is, the word of God, which is at work in you believers.* 1 Thessalonians 2:13

In your own words, what did the Thessalonian believers do right?

The Bible will maintain its miraculous status as the Word of God whether we accept it or reject it; that's a given. But if we refuse to accept the Bible as truth spoken by God, we can only experience it as judgment on our attitudes and actions in life. On the other hand, when we accept the Bible as God's Word, as the believers in Thessalonica did, we allow it to work in our lives.

In other words, the Bible isn't affected by our acceptance, but we are certainly altered by accepting the Bible as the Word of God.

How would a person behave who had actively accepted that everything written in the Bible is truth spoken directly by God?

Do you behave that way? Explain your answer.

This acceptance of God's Word affects both the preacher and his congregation. The truth he delivers to others must be applied first as God's Word in his own life. In addition, the congregation must recognize in his demeanor and words a profound acknowledgment of God's Word that has affected him before he asks them to let it affect them. In other words, the preacher must be authentic and trustworthy. He should be able to share how he's been convicted and corrected by the Scriptures. He should let those who are listening sense the joy of discovering a rich truth that he stumbled over like a treasure hidden in a field (see Matt. 13:44).

At the same time, each individual and the congregation as a whole must choose to submit to the Bible as God's Word. When we study or listen to the Word, we should anticipate the moment we will hear God speak to us through His Word and by His Spirit. We must be still, alert, and responsive. We must reject the kind of ignorance and separation from the Word of God that was the condition of the people in Samuel's day. If we remain open to God's Word, we'll be ready to respond as Samuel did: "Speak, for your servant hears!" (1 Sam. 3:10).

Are you open to hearing from God through preaching experiences and reading His Word? How can you tell?

Do you expect to hear from God when you listen to a sermon or read a passage of Scripture? Why or why not?

Identify some practical steps you can take to increase your acceptance of God's Word and your anticipation to hear from the Lord during corporate worship as well as private study.

APPLYING THE WORD OF GOD

TODAY'S SCRIPTURE FOCUS   >

"Be doers of the word, and not hearers only,

deceiving yourselves." James 1:22

Most people in North America drive a car as a regular part of their week. Using automobiles to get from point A to point B to point C has been ingrained in our culture for decades. But there are certain people who've gone beyond using their cars to loving their cars. They enjoy cleaning out engine components, checking tire pressures, and adding fluids.

Whether you love your car or just drive it around, you've probably had some experience with the owner's manual that came with it. People who love cars get excited about the manual because it acquaints them more intimately with the distinctive specifications of the vehicle. Those who just drive their cars, on the other hand, read the manual only to get basic facts and to avoid making mistakes.

Many people have described the Bible as a kind of owner's manual for those who wish to live as disciples of Jesus Christ, and there's a lot to be said for that analogy. Yesterday we looked at four ways the Scriptures are profitable in our lives: teaching, reproof, correction, and training in righteousness. Those four categories are similar to what you'll find in the owner's manual of a car.

1. Teaching connects with the specifications and vehicle history.
2. Reproof connects with the various warnings, cautions, and "idiot lights."
3. Correction connects with the diagnoses and troubleshooting portions of the manual.
4. Training in righteousness connects with the vehicle's recommended maintenance.

What are some of the unfortunate things that can happen when we fail to consult the owner's manual for our vehicles?

What can happen when we don't consult the owner's manual for our lives?

Both biblical preaching and personal Bible study expose us to God's Word, giving us opportunities to listen to what His Word says specifically to us. Once we hear what the Holy Spirit wants to communicate through a text, we must then accept that what we've heard comes from God—that it carries the authority of God and therefore has the power to change our lives.

After we hear the truth and accept its authority, we're then responsible to apply that truth to our lives.

HEARING AND DOING

Let's start with a definition. Application is the process of internalizing and acting on the truth of God's Word. The Scriptures are timeless in their relevance and applicability; application is a timely connection between the truth of God's Word and the changes required in our lives.

In Today's Scripture Focus the apostle James cuts to the bone when it comes to applying the truths of God's Word: "Be doers of the word, and not hearers only, deceiving yourselves" (Jas. 1:22).

Describe what it would look like for someone to be only a hearer of God's Word. How would that play out in everyday life?

What are characteristics of people who are "doers of the word"?

It's vitally important to understand: after you hear a sermon and/or read a portion of Scripture, nothing significant happens in your life until you act on what you've heard. It doesn't matter if you're blown away by a particular verse or concept. It makes no difference if you're seized with conviction about a specific sin. Unless you take action, your opportunity to experience life-change and transformation will end before it even got started.

We talked earlier about serving as a herald of God's Word—that we all have the responsibility to proclaim the truths of Scripture, whether or not we preach every weekend. But such heralding is effective only when our proclamation is supported by our actions.

Think of a time when you were struck by an insight or convicted of your sin but took no action afterward. What prevented you from taking action?

What impact did that insight or conviction ultimately have on your life?

How can you more effectively apply the truths of God's Word you encounter through preaching and personal study?

UNAPOLOGETIC APPLICATION

I have pastor friends who shy away from including steps for application in their sermons because they want to avoid legalistic to-do lists or because they have an aversion to imposing personal convictions on other people. This is unfortunate.

The reality is that several passages of God's Word, including Today's Scripture Focus, command us to apply scriptural truth in our lives and to help others engage in application as well.

Read the following passages of Scripture and record what they communicate about the necessity of application.

Matthew 25:31-46

John 14:12-17

James 2:18-26

A biblical sermon should lead to at least one crucial application question or step the audience can grapple with. That was the case when Peter preached the church's first sermon. It remains true today.

Read Acts 2:36-41. In your own words, what application step did Peter recommend to his hearers?

What was the result?

Peter boldly proclaimed the gospel of Jesus Christ. Look at the way the people responded: "Brothers, what shall we do?" (Acts 2:37). That's a question every preacher should hope for and be prepared to answer. Peter certainly was. He didn't say, "Sorry, I can't tell you what you must do; the Holy Spirit has to give you that answer." Rather, he provided an immediate recommendation for application: "Repent and be baptized every one of you in the name of Jesus Christ of the forgiveness of your sins, and you will receive the gift of the Holy Spirit" (v. 38).

God wrote an entire book filled with application—packed with actions He intended His people to take. And because His Word is authoritative, we can preach, read, and apply these actions with confidence.

Now we need to understand that application is hard work. It's taxing for preachers because it requires us to ask, "What does God want me to apply from this passage to my own life?" But application isn't only for preachers. That same question should be on your mind every time you open God's Word or listen to a sermon.

To practice the process of application, read James 1:2-18 and answer the following questions in connection with those verses.

Teaching: What doctrines or concepts can I learn from this passage?

Reproof: What behaviors or beliefs do I need to repent of?

Correction: What corrective steps do I need to take in order to change those behaviors or beliefs?

Training in righteousness: How can I begin to engage in the healthy behaviors and beliefs this passage recommends?

James 1:22 is a popular verse, but James wasn't finished after admonishing us to be doers of the Word instead of hearers only. He had some other things to say:

> *If anyone is a hearer of the word and not a doer, he is like a man*
> *who looks intently at his natural face in a mirror. For he looks at himself*
> *and goes away and at once forgets what he was like. But the one who looks*
> *into the perfect law, the law of liberty, and perseveres, being no hearer who*
> *forgets but a doer who acts, he will be blessed in his doing.* James 1:23-25

What do you think James meant by "the law of liberty" (v. 25)?

When have you been blessed in your attempts to apply God's Word?

If your focus is merely on the natural person—on your own efforts to change your behavior—you won't experience lasting impact. But when you look at the perfect Word of God, you focus on spiritual truth that brings freedom. And by putting that truth into action, you allow the Word to transform your life.

Don't stop at hearing and learning the Word. Only applying it can bring the transformation and new life that you so desperately need.

Day 5 /

APPRECIATING THE WORD OF GOD

TODAY'S SCRIPTURE FOCUS   >

"Oh how I love your law! It is my meditation all the day."

Psalm 119:97

If you want to follow a healthful diet, you need to eat healthful foods at almost every meal. That makes sense, right? I can't eat hamburgers and french fries for breakfast, lunch, and dinner and then hope a carrot will make my stomach feel better when I start to get sick. That's not how it works.

Rather, a healthful approach to eating means I eat fruits and vegetables every day. It means I limit the amount of fat and sugar I allow in my body. It means I buy whole-grain bread instead of the stuff that looks like Styrofoam™. Those kinds of habits build a foundation for a healthful lifestyle.

When we think about spiritual health, it works the same way. We don't help ourselves by skipping church for three weeks out of the month and then downloading a couple sermons as podcasts. Neither do we receive much benefit by opening our Bibles on Sunday and keeping them closed for the remainder of the week. People who are spiritually healthy intentionally expose themselves to the Word of God through personal study and unapologetic preaching. They listen to what God's Word has to say about their lives. They accept the authority of the Scriptures. And they work to apply what they've heard by bending their attitudes and actions to match the truths of those Scriptures.

When followers of Jesus commit to that kind of spiritual lifestyle on a regular basis, they begin to truly appreciate God's Word as a primary source of sustenance for their everyday lives.

What's your reaction to the previous ideas for maintaining spiritual health through God's Word? Why?

Do you currently have a spiritually healthful lifestyle? Explain your answer.

WORDS OF LIFE

One of the interesting things about Jesus' public ministry is that whenever the crowds started getting too large, He said or did something seemingly outrageous to shake off the chaff—to get rid of the people who only wanted to see a show but weren't interested in dedicating their lives to His kingdom. That's what happened in John 6.

Read John 6:52-69. How would you summarize Jesus' teaching in these verses?

How would you summarize Peter's response when Jesus asked, "Do you want to go away as well?" (v. 67).

The apostle Peter had his shortcomings; there's no doubt about that. But he sure nailed it when Jesus asked whether the disciples wanted to abandon ship with the rest of the crowd: "Lord, to whom shall we go? You have the words of eternal life, and we have believed, and have come to know, that you are the Holy One of God" (vv. 68-69).

Peter understood that following Jesus wasn't about finding a message he may or may not agree with, nor was it about avoiding difficult situations. It was about being with Him. Peter realized that Jesus alone was the source of eternal life and the answer to what he'd been searching for his entire life.

Also notice the progression in Peter's words. The disciples heard "the words of eternal life" from Jesus, and they caused the disciples to believe. But after living with Jesus day after day, the disciples had "come to *know*" that Jesus is the Holy One of God. Their regular, sustaining experiences with Christ had solidified their intellectual belief into something stronger and more permanent.

How do you most often experience Jesus' presence? How often do you experience it?

Where are you currently on the progression from hearing Jesus' words to believing Him to *knowing* He's your source of life every day?

WORSHIP AND THE WORD

When I reflect on the four pillars that make up the life of a vertical church—adoration, preaching, witness, and prayer—it's difficult to think of them in any kind of prioritized sequence. Worshiping God and preaching His Word function in such harmony that they can be separated only for examination. The Word of God informs and directs our worship, and worship awakens, deepens, and satisfies our hunger to hear God's Word. Witnessing and prayer occur throughout worship and preaching. It all works together under God's sovereign management.

That being the case, whether you're the speaker or a listener during preaching experiences on the weekend, your daily time in God's Word must be personal and delightful in order for you to maintain spiritual health. If you aren't regularly nourishing yourself in God's Word, don't expect a sermon by itself to accomplish that task.

The Scriptures must be more than a mine where you go looking for sermonic diamonds or spiritual bytes. As you regularly and consistently consume God's Word, it will become a place you long to visit because of what happens in you and to you when you're there.

I love the way David expresses these ideas throughout the longest chapter in the Bible, Psalm 119:

Teach me, O LORD, the way of your statutes;
and I will keep it to the end.
Give me understanding, that I may keep your law
and observe it with my whole heart.
Lead me in the path of your commandments,
for I delight in it.
Incline my heart to your testimonies,
and not to selfish gain!
Turn my eyes from looking at worthless things;
and give me life in your ways. Psalm 119:33-37

David summarized his delight in and appreciation for God's Word in Today's Scripture Focus:

Oh how I love your law!
It is my meditation all the day. Psalm 119:97

How has exposure to biblical preaching deepened your love for God's Word? List specific examples.

How has your personal time in Bible study deepened your love for God's Word?

What do you hope to accomplish or experience in the near future that will continue to deepen your love for God's Word?

It's a simple formula: spending time in the Scriptures deepens our appreciation for God and leads us to worship Him. And that's the foundation for spiritual health.

Read Nehemiah 8:1-12. Record three ways the Israelites demonstrated an appreciation for God's Word.

I said earlier that I'm a realist when it comes to sermons. So whenever I preach, I recognize that people won't remember my outline three weeks, three months, or three years from now. I get that.

What I try to do is start a fresh fire in listeners' hearts that will burn for a week. That's all I'm going for. No matter the Scripture passage or the subject, my message is the same: "Go live for Jesus Christ. Give Him everything. You'll never regret it. He's worth giving your life for. You'll never be disappointed with what you've given to Him."

I want to encourage people to press forward and live for Jesus: "For this I toil, struggling with all his energy that he powerfully works within me" (Col. 1:29). That's what preaching is about.

What's your reaction to those statements? How can you pray for your pastor this week?

What's your responsibility to prepare for and respond to the sermon each week?

What's your responsibility in becoming a student who appreciates God's Word?

I pray that you will become a believer whose "delight is in the law of the LORD" and who meditates on His law day and night (Ps. 1:2). I pray that faithfully sitting under the consistent preaching of God's Word will increase your appreciation for the Scriptures and your delight in God Himself. I pray that developing personal habits of Bible study will reinforce what you're being taught and that you'll check what you hear against the truth of the Bible.

Please hear me and believe what I say: the more you delight in and appreciate God's Word, the more you'll realize that it's a never-ending wellspring of nourishment that will bless you beyond measure.

1. Thayer and Smith, "Greek Lexicon entry for Kēryssō," *The New Testament Greek Lexicon* [online, cited 8 June 2012]. Available from the Internet: *www.biblestudytools.com.*

2. Darrell L. Bock, "Galatians," in *The Bible Knowledge Word Study: Acts–Ephesians* (Colorado Springs: Victor, 2006), 377. Available from the Internet: *http://books.google.com.*

3. Eugene Peterson, *Eat This Book* (Grand Rapids: William B. Eerdmans Publishing Co.), 71.

WHAT BRINGS THE GLORY DOWN

UNAFRAID WITNESS

WEEK SEVEN

START

Welcome back to this small-group discussion of *Vertical Church*.

The application challenge from the previous session involved researching and writing a sermon outline. How did it go?

What did you find surprising about the experience of writing a sermon? What did you enjoy?

What did you like best from week 6 in the workbook? What questions do you still have?

How do you hope to grow as a participant in preaching experiences? In your personal study of God's Word?

To prepare to view the DVD segment, read these verses aloud.

> *Peter, filled with the Holy Spirit, said to them, "Rulers of the people and elders, if we are being examined today concerning a good deed done to a crippled man, by what means this man has been healed, let it be known to all of you and to all the people of Israel that by the name of Jesus Christ of Nazareth, whom you crucified, whom God raised from the dead—by him this man is standing before you well. This Jesus is the stone that was rejected by you, the builders, which has become the cornerstone. And there is salvation in no one else, for there is no other name under heaven given among men by which we must be saved."*
>
> *Now when they saw the boldness of Peter and John, and perceived that they were uneducated, common men, they were astonished. And they recognized that they had been with Jesus.*
> Acts 4:8-13

WATCH

Complete the viewer guide below as you watch DVD session 7.

You can have your sin washed away and _____ by a holy God by placing your _____ in Jesus Christ, who took the punishment for your sin upon Himself.

God's work of salvation _____ _____ witness.

Only God can save a person, but He has decided that He wants to do that work through _____.

Some will _____ our witness and be _____.

The main thing that ripens a person to the gospel is the _____ of life.

Some will _____ our witness and _____.

If you're not willing to be the fragrance of _____ to those who are perishing, you can never be the fragrance of _____ to those who are being saved.

Human response to our witness produces _____.

God's work of salvation _____ _____ witness.

A bold witness is a simple, direct, sincere statement of _____ about Christ.

As your _____ for Christ goes up, your _____ to tell other people about Him goes up.

Techniques of human persuasion are _____.

Bold witness is _____.

RESPOND

Discuss the DVD segment with your group, using the questions below.

> What did you find most interesting about the DVD segment? Why?

> What emotions do you experience when you hear the word *evangelism?* Why?

> Describe your most positive experience with evangelism in recent years. What happened, and why is it important to you?

> In your own words, what's the difference between a red apple and a green apple?

> What's your reaction to the idea that some people are ripe to the gospel, while others aren't? Why?

> What's your reaction to this statement? "If you're not willing to be the fragrance of death to those who are perishing, you can never be the fragrance of life to those who are being saved."

> What does it mean to be a bold witness for the gospel of Jesus? What does it look like in practical terms for Christians to demonstrate boldness in their everyday lives?

APPLICATION

Before you conclude this time of discussion, make a list of five persons you believe to be red apples. Commit to pray every day this week that they will hear a bold declaration of the gospel.

SCRIPTURE MEMORY FOR THIS WEEK

We are not, like so many, peddlers of God's word, but as men of sincerity,
as commissioned by God, in the sight of God we speak in Christ.
2 Corinthians 2:17

READ WEEK 7 AND COMPLETE THE ACTIVITIES BEFORE THE NEXT GROUP EXPERIENCE.

WEEK 7

"We are not, like so many, peddlers of God's word, but as men of sincerity, as commissioned by God, in the sight of God we speak in Christ."

2 Corinthians 2:17

SAY IT IN A SENTENCE   >

Clear, direct witness to others about your relationship with Jesus Christ brings the glory down.

THE PLAGUE AND THE CURE >

You've probably heard of the Black Plague, but you may not be fully aware of its consequences in the ancient world. More than one hundred million people died in the pandemic, including nearly half the populations of great cities like Paris and London. The Black Plague decimated the human race and altered the course of world history.

Today we know the disease was spread by a lethal combination of rats and fleas, but the people experiencing the plague had no idea. Doctors told people to breathe the aroma of flowers and carry petals in their pockets in the hopes that breathing something good would displace the disease. Even worse, people dying in hospital beds were fed spoonfuls of ashes to induce coughing. The hope was that an afflicted person would spew out the secret source of slaughter. You've probably heard the macabre children's rhyme that was written in response to supposed remedies that never worked:

Ring around the roses
A pocket full of posies
Ashes, ashes
We all fall down.

Why do I mention this? Because a much more potent affliction has been ravaging the world for thousands of years: sin.

We began this study by looking at the universal longing in every human heart, a longing implanted in us by our Creator God that can't be satisfied or suppressed by any aroma of human experience. Sexual experimentation and substance abuse only make us sicker. Spoonfuls of status or acquiring stuff to satiate this hunger inevitably lead to vomiting what we foolishly ingest as we search in vain for fulfillment. People all around us experience the same searching, the inability to find what they need, and the spewing that follows every failed attempt until "we all fall down."

The world needs the gospel in order to be cured, and Christ followers have a part to play in meeting that need.

Day 1 /
THE KEY WORD IS *BOLDNESS*

TODAY'S SCRIPTURE FOCUS   >

"When they saw the boldness of Peter and John, and perceived that they were uneducated, common men, they were aston-ished. And they recognized that they had been with Jesus."

Acts 4:13

Start your study this week by thinking of a few words or phrases that cause you to instantly experience fear. We all have that kind of reaction, although different people respond to different words. For example, high-school students may react with fear when they hear the phrase *pop quiz*. Accountants may break out in a cold sweat when they hear they word *audit*. And middle-aged men carrying a few extra pounds may become instantly terrified when they hear the word *diet*.

What words cause you to experience instant fear? Record three.

1.

2.

3.

I think many Christians experience a pang of fear whenever they hear the word *evangelism*. As followers of Jesus, we know we're supposed to share the gospel with other people, but we don't always know how or when to do so—or even why it's important in the first place. As a result, our attempts at witnessing become stale and fruitless.

What emotions do you experience when you hear the word *evangelism*?

If you had to use one word to summarize your recent experiences with evangelism, what would it be? Why?

Contrary to popular opinion, God has done more than give us good news He wants to spread. He's given us a manner that must accompany every method and a rationale for that manner. The single term that best describes the way God wants His gospel disseminated is *boldness*.

A BOLD WITNESS

The word *parrhesia* is used 42 times in the New Testament. It's translated in several different ways, including *openly*, *freely*, *plainly*, and *with confidence*. But the most common translation is some form of the word *bold*.

A bold witness isn't a pushy witness. A bold witness isn't a loud witness, unless it needs to be. Boldness isn't obnoxiousness. It isn't rude or demanding. Boldness is the furthest thing from some wild-eyed preacher screeching in the streets, "You're going to hell!"

Boldness is clear, direct communication in the face of potential opposition—nothing more or less.

About which subjects are you able to speak boldly? What's the source of your confidence about those subjects?

When have you spoken boldly about the gospel? What happened?

BOLD DISCIPLES

One of my favorite examples of this kind of boldness comes from Acts 4. Recall that in Acts 2 Peter's sermon on the Day of Pentecost resulted in more than three thousand people joining the church. In Acts 3 Peter and John healed a crippled man who was known to everyone because he begged every day in front of the temple. The religious leaders in Jerusalem got mad about the hoopla that surrounded these events—they thought they'd already put an end to the whole Jesus thing—so they arrested Peter and John at the beginning of Acts 4 and commanded them to explain themselves.

Here's what Peter said in response:

> *Rulers of the people and elders, if we are being examined today concerning*
> *a good deed done to a crippled man, by what means this man has been healed,*
> *let it be known to all of you and to all the people of Israel that by the name*
> *of Jesus Christ of Nazareth, whom you crucified, whom God raised from the*
> *dead—by him this man is standing before you well. This Jesus is the stone*
> *that was rejected by you, the builders, which has become the cornerstone.*
> *And there is salvation in no one else, for there is no other name*
> *under heaven given among men by which we must be saved.* Acts 4:8-12

Now that's bold! And it's clear from Today's Scripture Focus that Peter and John's boldness was apparent (and impressive) even to those who despised them: "When they saw the boldness of Peter and John, and perceived that they were uneducated, common men, they were astonished. And they recognized that they had been with Jesus" (Acts 4:13).

Read Matthew 26:69-75. How would you describe Peter's actions in this passage?

How would you describe Peter, based on his actions recorded in Acts 4?

What changes in Peter could account for his drastically changed behavior?

PAUL'S BOLDNESS

Some suggest boldness is a matter of personality or preference, not binding on all Christians for all time. And in a way that makes sense; some people are just born with an extra level of boldness no matter what they're talking about, right?

However, I think Paul made it clear that boldness is not simply about personality when he wrote Ephesians 6:18-20:

> *To that end keep alert with all perseverance, making supplication*
> *for all the saints, and also for me, that words may be given to me in opening*
> *my mouth boldly to proclaim the mystery of the gospel, for which I am*
> *an ambassador in chains, that I may declare it boldly, as I ought to speak.*

"Boldly, as I *ought* to speak" (emphasis added). Boldness isn't just a good way for people who happen to enjoy being bold. It's the right way, the God way, and the biblical method for talking to people about Jesus.

What's your reaction to the statements you just read?

Can you think of recent conversations or interactions when you should have spoken more boldly for Christ and the gospel? If so, what held you back?

Read the following passages of Scripture and record what they demonstrate about Paul's boldness in proclaiming the gospel.

Acts 9:18-31

Acts 13:1-12

Acts 14:19-23

THE BOLDNESS OF JESUS

Many people have tried to paint a picture of Jesus that reflects only His softer side. They view Jesus as a meek, gentle Teacher who asked a bunch of questions so that He wouldn't ruffle a lot of feathers.

That's not Jesus. Our Savior was bold. In fact, the disciples learned their boldness from watching Him. For example, Jesus made it clear that boldness means speaking plainly:

> *He began to teach them that the Son of Man must suffer many things*
> *and be rejected by the elders and the chief priests and the scribes and be*
> *killed, and after three days rise again. And he said this plainly.* Mark 8:31-32

That word *plainly* is the same one translated in other places as *boldness*. Boldness is simply speaking the gospel plainly. Christians shouldn't be afraid of speaking for Jesus because they think they need eloquence. Plainness of speech is all God requires. "God loves you. Jesus Christ died for you. He can change your life. He did it for me. He will do it for you." That's the kind of garden-variety, plain-old, blue-jean boldness God blesses.

When do you feel pressure to speak eloquently or elaborately when it comes to spiritual matters? What's the source of that pressure?

What steps can you take to speak more plainly about the gospel?

Jesus also made it clear that boldness means speaking openly: "Some of the people of Jerusalem therefore said, 'Is not this the man whom they seek to kill? And here he is, speaking *openly,* and they say nothing to him!' " (John 7:25-26, emphasis added).

Hide it under a bushel? No! Again we find the word often translated *boldness,* but here it's the idea of freely expressing truth as you see it. It's not preachy, arrogant, or force-feeding anything. It's open and forthright.

Boldness is the way you talk when you have an urgent message. If you were vacating a building because there was a fire on your floor and you met some people from your office walking toward the elevator, you wouldn't hesitate to freely express the danger of going in the wrong direction. Knowing they were unaware, you'd never consider withholding something they obviously needed to know.

Where do you feel restricted from speaking openly about the gospel?

What's the source of that restriction?

Jesus also taught that boldness means speaking clearly: "The hour is coming when I will no longer speak to you in figures of speech but will tell you *plainly* about the Father" (John 16:25, emphasis added). Again it's the same word, *boldness.* Jesus was declaring a time when figures of speech would be set aside in favor of plain, open, clear communication. And guess what: that time is now!

What spiritual concepts cause you to feel confused when you think about sharing with lost people?

Where can you go to gain greater clarity about those concepts?

I'm absolutely convinced that Jesus Christ is the only hope for fallen humanity. I trust you're convinced of that as well, and I hope you're willing to communicate that message in a way that is plain, open, clear, and—most of all—bold.

Day 2 /

THE RESULT IS FRAGRANT

TODAY'S SCRIPTURE FOCUS   >

"Thanks be to God, who in Christ always leads us in triumphal procession, and through us spreads the fragrance of the knowledge of him everywhere. For we are the aroma of Christ to God among those who are being saved and among those who are perishing, to one a fragrance from death to death, to the other a fragrance from life to life. Who is sufficient for these things?"

2 Corinthians 2:14-16

Do you have a favorite fragrance? I'm not necessarily talking about perfume or cologne, although both qualify as options. I'm asking what smells make you smile as soon as you encounter them. Maybe it's the aroma of brewing coffee, for example. Maybe it's a particular food or flower.

What are your favorite smells? List three.

1.

2.

3.

Why are we talking about smells? Because that's one of the metaphors regularly used in Scripture to describe our interaction with God, starting all the way back with Noah and the ark:

Noah built an altar to the L<small>ORD</small> and took some of every clean animal and some of every clean bird and offered burnt offerings on the altar. And when the L<small>ORD</small> smelled the pleasing aroma, the L<small>ORD</small> said in his heart, "I will never again curse the ground because of man, for the intention of man's heart is evil from his youth. Neither will I ever again strike down every living creature as I have done."
Genesis 8:20-21

God doesn't need food. He wasn't pleased by the aroma of Noah's sacrifice in the same way we're pleased when we smell steaks cooking on the grill. Rather, He was pleased by what Noah's offering represented. God was gratified by Noah's obedience and worship, which are represented as a "pleasing aroma" (v. 21).

Read the following verses and record what else you learn about God's response to our obedience and worship.

Exodus 29:15-18

Leviticus 26:27-31

Ezekiel 20:40-44

The Bible also connects this metaphor of aroma with incense as a way of representing the prayers of God's people. Look at Revelation 8, for example:

Another angel came and stood at the altar with a golden censer, and he was given much incense to offer with the prayers of all the saints on the golden altar before the throne, and the smoke of the incense, with the prayers of the saints, rose before God from the hand of the angel. Revelation 8:3-4

What words and images do you find interesting in these verses? Why?

Why is the burning of incense a good metaphor for our prayers?

THE AROMA OF CHRIST

In Today's Scripture Focus Paul used a similar metaphor when he wrote to encourage the members of the church in Corinth:

> *Thanks be to God, who in Christ always leads us in triumphal procession, and through us spreads the fragrance of the knowledge of him everywhere. For we are the aroma of Christ to God among those who are being saved and among those who are perishing, to one a fragrance from death to death, to the other a fragrance from life to life. Who is sufficient for these things?* 2 Corinthians 2:14-16

What are the key images in these verses?

Who is the focus of these verses—Christ or we? Explain your answer.

Let's dig deeper into some of the key phrases from those verses, starting with "triumphal procession" (v. 14). In the days of the Roman Empire, the army was given a celebratory parade through the streets of Rome whenever it won a significant battle. The general or commander of the army typically led these processions by riding along in a chariot, and the soldiers carried in all the treasure, slaves, and other spoils of war they'd collected from their victory.

These parades were attended by thousands of people who watched from the streets. The crowd would cheer and shout their appreciation for the army. They'd also burn incense and throw thousands of flowers in front of the procession, which, when crushed by the horses and chariots, produced an explosion of aromas. That's the idea Paul had in mind when he wrote that we are "the fragrance of the knowledge of him" (v. 14) and "the aroma of Christ" (v. 15).

Paul used that aromatic explosion as a metaphor for evangelism—for the spread of the gospel. If you've ever cut open an orange or dabbed a little too much cologne on your hands, you know how quickly and powerfully a fragrance can diffuse through the air and spread across a room. That's how it's supposed to work when the good news spreads throughout the world.

What metaphor would you use to describe the way the gospel is spreading in your community? In the world? Explain your answer.

GOD AND US

Note two things Paul emphasized. First, it's "always" Christ (v. 14) who leads the triumphal procession. The most important thing we need to know about evangelism is that God, and only God, is the catalyst for spiritual transformation. God alone convicts us of our sin. God alone changes hearts. God alone brings salvation.

That's a point Paul continued to make in his letter to the Corinthians, including this verse: "We all, with unveiled face, beholding the glory of the Lord, are being transformed into the same image from one degree of glory to another. For this comes from the Lord who is the Spirit" (2 Cor. 3:18).

What's your reaction to the idea that God is the only source of spiritual transformation? Why?

Read the following passages of Scripture and record how they contribute to your understanding of God's role in our salvation.

John 14:1-6

Romans 5:1-2

Ephesians 2:8-9

The second thing Paul emphasized is that God chooses to spread the fragrance of the gospel "through us" (2 Cor. 2:14). So Christ is the leader, but we're in the procession. God alone can save a person, but somehow, for some reason, He's chosen to accomplish that work of salvation "through us."

Are you glad God wants to use us to spread the message of His gospel? Why or why not?

How are you currently letting God use you to accomplish His work of salvation in the world?

DEATH AND LIFE

Let's take a look at the second half of Today's Scripture Focus: "We are the aroma of Christ to God among those who are being saved and among those who are perishing, to one a fragrance from death to death, to the other a fragrance from life to life" (2 Cor. 2:15-16).

"A fragrance from death to death" (v. 16). That seems like a bit of a downer, right? But it's reality. Jesus Christ is the aroma of death to those who are perishing. He reminds people of their ultimate fate and of their eternal destiny without Him. He reveals the sinful nature within us and the rotting, putrid stench of our lives when we attempt to live separated from Him.

So Paul's point to the Corinthians—and to all of us—is that you can't have it both ways. If you're going to be used by God as a witness to the gospel, you're going to stink to a lot of people who've rejected that gospel. Christ is a stench to those who are dying in their sins, and so are we. It's *unavoidable!*

> **When have you felt like "a fragrance from death to death" because of the gospel? What emotions did you experience at the time?**

> **Are you willing to be a stench to many people in order to be used by Jesus? Why or why not?**

That's not the end of the story, though. Paul also reminds us we're "a fragrance from life to life" (v. 16) for those who are prepared to receive the message of the gospel. Just think about that for a moment. We're privileged to be witnesses in the process by which people we know and care about receive the gift of eternal life. In spite of our fumbling and our mistakes and our fear, we get to be involved in a momentous blessing!

> **When have you felt like "a fragrance from life to life" because of the gospel? What emotions did you experience at the time?**

You have an opportunity every day to participate in Jesus' work and mission in this world. And I hope you'll seize that opportunity with boldness and passion. Because unless you're willing to be the stench of death to those who are perishing, you'll never be the aroma of life to those who are being saved.

Day 3 /

WHY EVANGELISM OFTEN FAILS

TODAY'S SCRIPTURE FOCUS >

"We are not, like so many, peddlers of God's word,

but as men of sincerity, as commissioned by God,

in the sight of God we speak in Christ". 2 Corinthians 2:17

Let's do a quick review of what we've explored this week.

1. God wants evangelism to happen in the world. He wants "the fragrance of the knowledge of him" to spread, and He wants it to spread "everywhere" (2 Cor. 2:14).

2. We're supposed to be involved in the process of evangelism. God has chosen to make Himself known to the world "through us" (v. 14).

3. We're most effective as witnesses when we declare the message of the gospel with boldness rather than fear.

Given all that, here some crucial questions: Why is evangelism failing today in the North American church? Why are we seeing fewer and fewer conversions? Why aren't people being baptized? Why is church attendance declining at an alarming rate? What's the weak link in the chain?

How would you answer those questions? Why?

Here's my take on our current dilemma. I don't think God is the problem. It's we. We're failing as witnesses in the world, and the reason we're failing is that we give ourselves too much credit in the process, forgetting "salvation belongs to the LORD" (Ps. 3:8), or we don't witness boldly because we're afraid of the consequences.

Remember, the overriding question in vertical church isn't "How can we be more effective in working for God?" It's "How can we remove the barriers that prevent God from doing what He desires?" Unfortunately, we in the church have erected a lot of barriers when it comes to outreach and evangelism.

Today we're going to start tearing down those barriers.

What barriers are preventing you from serving as an effective witness for the gospel? When and why were those barriers constructed?

PEDDLING THE GOSPEL

Evangelism was a new idea for the early church, and many of the first Christians experienced great success in sharing the gospel with those who needed to hear it. Yet it's clear from Paul's words in Today's Scripture Focus that several members of the fledgling faith had already gone off track: "We are not, like so many, peddlers of God's word, but as men of sincerity, as commissioned by God, in the sight of God we speak in Christ" (2 Cor. 2:17).

Paul's use of the word *peddlers* carries the same meaning as *hucksters* or *hawkers* in today's society. It's the idea of withholding information or distorting facts in order to convince someone.

God doesn't want us to talk about Jesus like a used-car salesman in a plaid suit. He doesn't want us selling Jesus like a late-night infomercial promising a tonic that will cure baldness. We grimace at the comparison because we immediately recognize the manner of communication can greatly cheapen the message. But that doesn't mean we always present Jesus the right way.

Christians in Paul's day had adopted strategies and techniques to avoid being the aroma of death to people. They thought, *If I target someone and boldly share Christ, they get upset. So I've got to find an approach that doesn't upset anyone.*

That's why Paul wrote these words later in that same letter to the Corinthian church:

> *Having this ministry by the mercy of God, we do not lose heart.*
> *But we have renounced disgraceful, underhanded ways.*
> *We refuse to practice cunning or to tamper with God's word,*
> *but by the open statement of the truth we would commend ourselves*
> *to everyone's conscience in the sight of God.* 2 Corinthians 4:1-2

Why are people often tempted to soften the message of the gospel?

Have you ever been tempted to use cunning or subtlety to communicate the message of the gospel? If so, what was the result?

Sadly, the practice of peddling the gospel didn't stop with the early church. It continues today. Let's take a look at four evangelistic techniques, still prevalent in the church, that often turn well-meaning Christians into hucksters.

THE RELATIONAL GOSPEL

This is the idea that people will receive the gospel once they become your friends. Popularized in the 1970s by the book *Friendship Evangelism*, this method has been so broadly circulated in the Western world that it's considered to be irrefutably effective.

Make friends. Take them to baseball games. Wait for them to drop their guard and regard you as a confidant. Then somewhere down the road—a week, a month, a year, a decade from now—you'll earn the right to share Christ, and maybe they'll be saved. But either way you won't lose the relationship.

Have you used friendship evangelism in the past? What were the results?

In thousands of baptisms our church has witnessed, I can't recall hearing the friendship-evangelism story. Oh sure, "Somebody invited me to church" or "A friend reached out in my time of need and shared the gospel"—I've heard countless versions of those. But the "Jesus guy sees stranger; befriends him or her for the purpose of sharing Christ; earns the right through extended servanthood and exemplary love over a long period of time; and then that stranger, facing no personal crisis of any kind, chooses Jesus just because of the guy's compelling example"—that's a testimony I haven't heard.

I'm not saying it's never happened. I'm saying it's not typical, it's not biblical, it's not bold, and it's not working very well in the Western church.

That's because the power of the gospel is not in the relational capacity of the witness but in the message itself. Friendship evangelism, lifestyle evangelism, relational evangelism—all of it flows from our desire to avoid what can't be avoided. I'll say it again: if you aren't willing to be the stench of death to those who are perishing, you can't be the aroma of life to those who are being saved. The idea of having conversations with someone for months or years to earn the right to talk to him or her about Jesus betrays an elevation of the role of human persuasion in evangelism that doesn't square with the Gospels or the Book of Acts.

Do you agree with the assertion that relational evangelism isn't biblical and effective? Why or why not?

Is a Christian being a friend by withholding the gospel? Why or why not?

THE RENOWN GOSPEL

This is the idea that people will receive Christ because impressive people do. According to this method, a celebrity or public figure professes faith in Christ and experiences a surge in popularity as churches seek to capitalize on the person's fame and boost attendance by having him or her speak. Sadly, the sudden rise to Christian-celebrity status takes the novice convert to places where he or she is vulnerable to disillusionment, and departure from the Christian phase comes too often and too quickly.

How have you seen this type of evangelism play out in recent years? How have you been affected by it personally?

In your experience what kind of fruit does this celebrity evangelism produce?

Here's the truth: we can't impress people into salvation. That's peddling God's Word. I understand it's usually well intentioned, but it ends up being manipulative and hurtful to those struggling with sin and all Jesus came to save us from.

A faithful witness to the gospel elevates Christ, not His representatives. Jesus doesn't need PR; He needs proclamation. Vertical church isn't about God sitting by and watching us convince people they need Jesus to improve their horizontal world. God is the seeker, and when we boldly proclaim Jesus, it provokes Him to show up in saving power and conquer the horizontal idols that hold human hearts.

THE REASONABLE GOSPEL

This idea says people should receive Christ because it makes sense or it's easy. This is a particularly insidious argument because the message of the gospel is indeed simple, but it's by no means easy to live out.

When we replace boldness with blandness, we get light on repentance and too quick in delivery. Getting saved isn't a drive-through or a drive-by experience. And in my experience the Four Spiritual Laws, the Roman Road, Steps to Peace with God, and other formulas that seek to make the gospel accessible usually run the risk of being superficial. Jesus never hid the cost of following Him, and it is great sin when we do.

Do you agree with the assertion that a generic gospel presentation can be superficial? Why or why not?

Have you used some form of the reasonable gospel in the past? What were the results?

We must hold to the simplicity of the gospel without hurrying the decision or hiding the cost. The gospel costs a person everything; Jesus calls us to deny ourselves, take up our cross, and follow Him (see Luke 9:23). Jesus is the celebrated guest at the greatest banquet of all time and the treasure hidden in a field. He demands that we give up everything for Him. We give up our sin for a Savior. We give up ourselves for a Master. We give up our hopes and dreams for His eternal purposes.

THE RESOURCE GOSPEL

This method says people should receive Christ because their lives will improve immensely: "Don't you want to be healthy? Don't you want to be wealthy? Don't you want to have paradise here on earth? Jesus Christ is the best investment you'll ever make. Put the Son of God in your portfolio, and your life will take off like a rocket."

How have you seen this type of evangelism play out in recent years? How have you been affected by it personally?

In your experience what kind of fruit does resource evangelism produce?

Even where the health-and-wealth gospel hasn't invaded the church, we can slip into a more subtle version of this error. Jesus Christ promises us a cross to carry, a sword in place of peace, and exacting accountability for those who claim Him as Lord. Assuring people of benefits Jesus doesn't promise or hiding the cost of following Him is a total departure from the gospel work revealed in Scripture.

Each of these erroneous gospel iterations was incubated in a sincere desire to see people saved. But when we want a decision for Christ more than we want a disciple, we get tares instead of true converts. We get Ichabod, departed glory for the church.

May it be so no longer in the body of Christ, and may you never build these kinds of barriers against the clear, bold, transformational work of Jesus.

Based on today's lesson, how does your approach to sharing the gospel need to change?

APPLES AND APPLES

TODAY'S SCRIPTURE FOCUS   >

"Do you not say, 'There are yet four months, then comes the harvest'? Look, I tell you, lift up your eyes, and see that the fields are white for harvest. Already the one who reaps is receiving wages and gathering fruit for eternal life, so that sower and reaper may rejoice together." John 4:35-36

My mom was the most effective personal evangelist I've ever known. During my childhood I often saw her sitting at our kitchen table, Bible open, engaged in earnest conversation with other women who lived on our street. Some of these women were friends, some became friends, and some remained friends though they didn't respond to the gospel. I never sensed my mother's friendship was a bargaining chip in evangelism. She found the biblical balance between influence and boldness.

Whom do you look up to and respect as an evangelist?

What characteristics make those people effective witnesses of the gospel?

In my attempts to wrestle through the ins and outs of evangelism, I've thought a lot about the women my mother reached for Christ, as well as about the women who refused the same messenger with the same message using the same bold method. In each instance when my mom was able to win and disciple a woman for Christ, an overarching life issue had ripened that woman's heart to the good news of Jesus. And I firmly believe understanding that kind of ripening is the key to effective evangelistic ministry in a vertical church.

Lest you think I've based a vertical understanding of evangelism entirely on my mom's pattern of witness, let me show it to you in God's Word. Today's Scripture Focus records Jesus' exhortation to every evangelist in His day and in the future, including you and me.

Reread Today's Scripture Focus. What words or phrases are most interesting to you? Why?

Rewrite these verses in your own words.

Please don't miss what Jesus was saying about the people He wants you and your church to reach with the good news. Here's what I see when I read these verses.

- Stop saying the harvest is months away; it's today.
- All around us at this moment, people are ripe to the gospel.
- Look past the preference of whom you want saved and locate those God has ripened.
- I can reap now where others have sown if I look for the ripe fruit.
- Gathering ripe fruit is reaping souls for eternal life.

Are you tracking with me? Those are vital principles for evangelism in a vertical church. Now let's look at what they mean practically for you.

RED AND GREEN

When speaking about theological ideas, I've always tried to adopt the most biblical and practical language possible. So when I think of evangelism, I refer to people who are ready to respond to the gospel as red apples; they're ripe to the good news. Similarly, I refer to people who aren't yet ready for the gospel as green apples.

Red and green. It may seem simplistic, but when you apply that filter to the way Jesus interacted with people, it changes the way you see the Gospels as well as gospel work today.

Jesus constantly cut through the crowds filled with green apples in order to focus His energy on the red ones already ripe for His message. He left a crowd of green apples to talk with Zacchaeus, for example (see Luke 19:1-10). He turned to a desperate woman with an issue of blood even though He was surrounded by masses of other people (see Luke 8:43-48). He talked at great length with Nicodemus, who longed for more than his formulaic religiosity (see John 3:1-21).

In every instance Jesus invested in the ripe red apples—those who were ready to abandon the life they knew for something better.

Read the following passages of Scripture and record ways they reflect this principle of red and green apples.

Matthew 15:21-28

Luke 8:26-39

John 5:1-17

Jesus gave unlimited time to the red apples He met, but He hardly acknowledged the green apples that crossed His path. Without insulting those who weren't ripe yet, He nonetheless refused their company and attention.

For example, when the rich young ruler approached Jesus, he asked, "What must I do to inherit eternal life?" (Mark 10:17). How many churches in our day would have that guy's name on a card or have him serving as an usher in a matter of minutes? But Jesus used the law to elicit the man's prideful assertion that he wasn't sinful: "All these I have kept from my youth" (v. 20). Christ responded, "Go, sell all that you have and give to the poor" (v. 21). Why did He say this? Not because divesting his wealth would gain the man eternal life, but because his refusal to do so revealed his unreadiness for any God other than the god of his possessions. He was a green apple.

Read Luke 9:57-62. How do these verses demonstrate Jesus' attitude toward green apples?

What's your reaction to the concept of red and green apples? Why?

Identify three red apples and three green apples in your life.

Jesus wasn't shy in explaining the rationale behind His choices. He said, "The Son of Man came to seek and to save the lost" (Luke 19:10). "There will be more joy in heaven over one sinner who repents than over ninety-nine righteous persons who need no repentance" (Luke 15:7). "Those who are well have no need of a physician, but those who are sick. I came not to call the righteous, but sinners" (Mark 2:17).

In each instance where people were too shallow, too superficial, and too slow, Jesus turned the green apples away. But when people had become aware of personal sin, open to complete life change, and humbled enough to see their needs, they were ripe, red, and ready for a gospel witness. Those were the ones Christ sought.

WHAT MAKES A PERSON RIPE?

By now I'm guessing you're thinking about the serious flaw in this whole apple thing: you're not Jesus. Neither am I. We don't have the ability to discern the thoughts and minds of the people around us, so how do we determine whether someone is a red or green apple?

I found the answer to that question by personally baptizing thousands of former red apples that are now members of God's kingdom. When you have spiritual conversations with that many people and ask how each one came to Christ, you quickly see a pattern emerge and engrave itself on your mind, because every person tells the same story.

"I was going along thinking I was too sexy for my shirt, and God dropped a boulder on my life." That's every adult conversion story I've heard in almost three decades of ministry. The label on the boulder may change, but apart from that, the stories are identical. For some it was a failed marriage, profound loss, or personal loneliness. For others it was a persistent addiction or an existential crisis or misery when they discovered everything they'd acquired couldn't fill the longing in their souls. For many it was simply the realization that the love they longed for didn't come in a horizontal human package but only from a vertical source, and the weight of sin they carried could be lifted only by a Savior.

What kinds of boulders has God dropped on your life?

How did those circumstances prepare you to receive the gospel and draw closer to God?

God uses the circumstances of life to ripen people to the gospel. We can target people, take them to dinner, and testify through words and example of the truth about Jesus, but they'll remain green to the gospel. Only when God Himself moves in their hearts, ripening them through a situation or condition that bankrupts their own ability to solve their problems, will they respond to the gospel.

Therefore, look for the people around you who've been pinned down by boulders. Be aware of your friends and family members who've started to realize their best efforts at life just aren't cutting it.

Think about the people in your sphere of influence who are open to the gospel. What makes you recognize them as red apples? What life-altering circumstances are they dealing with?

What's holding you back from boldly presenting the gospel to those people?

When you find those people, be friendly. Be caring, compassionate, and empathetic about their needs. But most important, be bold in your presentation of the gospel and in your witness for Jesus Christ.

Day 5 /

WHAT TO DO WHILE YOU WAIT

TODAY'S SCRIPTURE FOCUS >

"Even if our gospel is veiled, it is veiled only to those who are perishing. In their case the god of this world has blinded the minds of the unbelievers, to keep them from seeing the light of the gospel of the glory of Christ, who is the image of God."

2 Corinthians 4:3-4

Nobody likes to wait, especially in Western culture. We want next-day shipping. We want high-speed Internet. We're willing to tolerate even mediocre fast food because there's almost no time between paying for our order and receiving our meal.

How do you feel about waiting? Why?

In what situations do you commonly get frustrated because you have to wait?

In contrast, God doesn't mind waiting. In fact, He often intentionally delays the fulfillment of something—even our most fervent prayers—to maintain His plan and His purposes. As Peter wrote, "Do not overlook this one fact, beloved, that with the Lord one day is as a thousand years, and a thousand years as one day" (2 Pet. 3:8).

That's good news when God demonstrates patience with our sin and rebellion. But it's bad news when we're waiting for someone we care about to ripen from a green apple into a red apple.

THE HARDEST PART

Waiting is hard for us. And it's especially agonizing for believers who long to see friends and family members experience salvation through Jesus Christ.

For example, a couple in our church are praying for their child in a same-sex relationship to repent and come home to family and to God. We have a wife praying for her husband who abandoned her and their four kids to dive headlong into his addiction. We have a man who got saved and longs to see his business partner come to faith in Christ and adopt high-integrity business practices.

In each of these situations and countless others like them, the pressure to see that person saved is immense. Every day of the struggle only increases the waiting Christian's pain and makes the lost person's salvation seem less likely. How can we stand it? What are we supposed to do while we wait?

Whom are you currently waiting for, hoping they'll be saved?

What emotions are you experiencing as you wait?

The first thing we can do is pray: "Do not be anxious about anything, but in everything by prayer and supplication with thanksgiving let your requests be made known to God" (Phil. 4:6). Worry won't accomplish anything. Frustration and anger will only do more damage. So pray.

Don't be passive, however, in your prayer. Don't just throw your hands up in the air and say, "God, Your will be done. I'm not going to think about it any longer." Pray fervently. Pray persistently. God honors that kind of intercession.

Read Luke 18:1-8. What does this parable teach us about God?

What does it teach us about prayer?

If you've already been praying and you don't feel anything good is happening in your loved one's life, be encouraged by the story of Saul.

Read Acts 9:1-9. What's your reaction to this story? Why?

What can we learn about God from Paul's encounter with Him?

What can we learn about salvation?

Saul was "breathing threats" (v. 1) against Christians, seeking to arrest, torture, and kill them. Then 10 minutes later he was taken to the mat and pinned by Jesus Christ Himself. Not only was Paul resistant to the gospel—a green apple—but he also seemed to be getting worse. It's not that Saul didn't see the truth and needed information. It's not that he refused to see the truth and needed confrontation. He couldn't see!

That's what it says in Today's Scripture Focus:

> *Even if our gospel is veiled, it is veiled only to those who are perishing.*
> *In their case the god of this world has blinded the minds of*
> *the unbelievers, to keep them from seeing the light of the gospel*
> *of the glory of Christ, who is the image of God.* 2 Corinthians 4:3-4

In the same way, the lost people you care about most might be closest to salvation when they are furthest from God. The key to recognizing those who are ripe is to see the signs that they are about to drop to one knee. Look for tears, a story of trauma, or a tired plea for strength they don't have.

Until then, refuse to cause additional damage while you wait. As we like to say in our church, "If you can't pick the fruit, don't bruise it." People get saved when God ripens their hearts. So if you've told your loved ones about Christ, the only next step is to pray and wait, love and pray.

While we wait for God to ripen the hearts of those we love, it's important that we don't get between the hammer (God) and the work (our loved ones).

What's your reaction to the ideas of praying and waiting for God to ripen your friend or loved one? Why?

Does this approach differ from what you've been doing? If so, how?

REAP A HARVEST

There's one other thing we can do while we wait for our loved ones to experience salvation: reap a harvest for God's kingdom by spending time with other people who are ready to receive salvation. Find the red apples in your job or on your street and boldly proclaim the gospel they desperately need to hear.

In other words, let God decide whom you evangelize and when you evangelize them. Release your loved ones into God's hands—He can take care of them, I assure you—and go minister in the areas to which you've been called.

Have you been neglecting red apples in your sphere of influence to concentrate your efforts on the people you love? In what ways?

What emotions do you experience when you think about releasing your loved one to God and ministering to others instead?

How sad when a Christian takes an unbelieving couple to dinner but fails to see and help the stranger crying in the bathroom of the restaurant. Pray for eyes to notice people like that. Talk to them; they know their way isn't working.

How unfortunate when we pray and plead for God to save our son, but we can't walk across the street and talk to the couple losing their house, their marriage, or their son to demonic darkness. Would God do more to ripen the hearts of those who are on our hearts if we did more to reach those already ripe who are on His heart?

How would you answer that question?

How blind we are to the guy in the office who's going to lose his job because of an addiction, personal pain, or pathetic performance. Take him to lunch and build a bridge to his gospel readiness. Can you see him ripening? How consistently we fail to recognize the people under a rock or up a tree and go to them with the message they are finally ripe to receive. Go hang out at Alcoholics Anonymous, for example; there you'll find a room full of ripe red apples—people looking to put flesh and bones on the "higher power" they acknowledge: *His name is Jesus.*

Jesus said the harvest is ready. We just need to open our eyes:

> **Jesus said to them, "My food is to do the will of him who sent me and to accomplish his work. Do you not say, 'There are yet four months, then comes the harvest'? Look, I tell you, lift up your eyes, and see that the fields are white for harvest. Already the one who reaps is receiving wages and gathering fruit for eternal life, so that sower and reaper may rejoice together."** John 4:34-36

Take a moment to pray, asking the Holy Spirit to reveal the harvest—the red apples—in your sphere of influence. Who are they? Where are they?

What can you do this week to begin boldly declaring the gospel where it's ready to be received?

The red apples are facing something, feeling something, needing something, searching for something—and you know the answer. So give it to them. And give it to them boldly.

WHAT BRINGS THE GLORY DOWN

UNCEASING PRAYER

WEEK EIGHT

START

Welcome back to this small-group discussion of *Vertical Church*.

The application challenge from the previous session involved praying for red apples to hear a bold declaration of the gospel. If you're comfortable, describe anything interesting or exciting that you experienced through those times of prayer.

What did you like best from week 7 of the workbook? What questions do you still have?

What have you appreciated most from this study so far? Why?

Are you currently satisfied or unsatisfied with your prayer life? If you're comfortable, explain your answer.

To prepare to view the DVD segment, read these verses aloud.

> *The word of the LORD came to Jeremiah a second time,*
> *while he was still shut up in the court of the guard:*
> *"Thus says the LORD who made the earth, the LORD who formed*
> *it to establish it—the LORD is his name: Call to me and*
> *I will answer you, and will tell you great*
> *and hidden things that you have not known."*
> Jeremiah 33:1-3

WATCH

Complete the viewer guide below as you watch DVD session 8.

_____: "Call to me" (Jer. 33:3).

If you have turned from your sin and embraced Jesus Christ by faith for your forgiveness, God has made a _____ with you.

God's invitation is for us to know Him _____.

You can _____ to the Creator of the universe, and He will _____ to you. And He wants you to!

The word _call_ is an expression of urgency, _____, fervency.

Scripture tells us not to think our prayers, not to whisper our prayers, not even to speak our prayers, but we are to _____ _____.

_____: "I will answer you" (Jer. 33:3).

ANSWERS GOD GIVES TO PRAYER

1. _____   2. _____   3. _____

_____: "I will tell you great ... things that you have not known" (Jer. 33:3).

Insight to understand what's happening and why comes through _____.

ENEMIES OF PRAYER

1. _____   2. _____   3. _____

_____: "I will tell you ... hidden things that you have not known" (Jer. 33:3).

God know things about our _____: great things, mighty things, hidden things.

_____ is what brings the glory down.

RESPOND

Discuss the DVD segment with your group, using the questions below.

> What did you like best about the DVD segment? Why?

> How did you feel about prayer when you were a child? Why?

> Growing up, what were your most common experiences with prayer? What are your most common experiences with prayer now?

> How do you react to this statement? "Scripture tells us not to think our prayers, not to whisper our prayers, not even to speak our prayers, but we are to call out."

> As a group, make a list of the different methods we can use when we pray. (Fasting is an example of a specific method.)

> When you don't receive something you've asked God for in prayer, what do you typically do next? What should we do?

> How can we overcome anger, fear, and doubt as obstacles to prayer?

APPLICATION

Look again at the list your group made of the different methods of prayer. Identify two methods you haven't practiced recently. Commit to approaching God regularly through those methods this week.

SCRIPTURE MEMORY FOR THIS WEEK

Thus says the LORD who made the earth, the LORD who formed it to establish it—the LORD is his name: Call to me and I will answer you, and will tell you great and hidden things that you have not known.
Jeremiah 33:2-3

READ WEEK 8 AND COMPLETE THE ACTIVITIES TO COMPLETE YOUR STUDY OF *VERTICAL CHURCH*.

WEEK 8

"Thus says the LORD who made the earth, the LORD who formed it to establish it—the LORD is his name: Call to me and I will answer you, and will tell you great and hidden things that you have not known."

Jeremiah 33:2-3

SAY IT IN A SENTENCE >

Fervent, faith-filled, persistent prayer is a prerequisite to God's manifest presence in a church.

BEFORE EVERYTHING ELSE >

My life has been filled with more blessings than I ever imagined possible. When I think about my family, my friends, and the opportunities we've shared in ministry together, I'm instantly filled with gratitude, even to the point of tears. I don't know how it all happened, but I'm certain I deserve none of it.

Here's what I do know: the foundation for everything I've experienced—the good times and the difficult times—has been prayer.

In 1986, when Kathy and I arrived in Chicago for two years of seminary and to take a position at a local church, the search committee for what would become Harvest Bible Chapel was already praying. Then, over the spring and summer of 1988, we began to meet in early-morning prayer meetings, late-night prayer vigils, and days and weeks of fasting and prayer. Before we were unapologetically preaching God's Word, unashamedly adoring God's Son, or sharing the gospel with boldness, we were persisting in fervent prayer.

What about you? When was the last time you participated in a faith-driven, expectation-filled prayer meeting that invited God to reveal His glory and show up with power at your church? I'm not talking about meetings in which one or two persons pray the will of God; I'm talking about a time when everyone in the room passionately agrees that God will replace their desperation with a manifestation of Himself. When that kind of prayer happens, God's will to save, heal, and restore is confidently petitioned by faith as people cry out to the Lord with a palpable sense of determined persistence.

Are you having experiences like that? You can. You should. And it's my goal in this final week to "stir you up by way of reminder" (2 Pet. 1:13) toward fervent, faith-filled, persistent prayer that brings down the glory of God.

Day 1 /

INVITATION

TODAY'S SCRIPTURE FOCUS >

"Thus says the LORD who made the earth, the LORD who formed it to establish it—the LORD is his name: Call to me and I will answer you, and will tell you great and hidden things that you have not known." Jeremiah 33:2-3

I've made no secret of my belief that the church in North America has experienced an epic failure in recent decades—a failure due to a lot of factors, many of which we've discussed in this study. But one of the primary causes of the church's decline has been our rejection of a vertical approach to prayer.

In my experience pastors and church leaders are not failing in prayer for lack of knowledge. It's not that we don't know about God's promises or the way He prioritizes prayer; it's simply that we don't do it. Failing in prayer, we wander further and further from the vertical-church vision. In our prayerlessness we seek to make cheap replicas of vertical results, and we use increasingly weird and increasingly fleshly horizontal methods of ministry.

Enough. Let's get back to a vertical approach to prayer so that we can see God move in awesome ways through our churches once again.

What's your reaction to the previous statements? Why?

Are you satisfied with your current experiences with prayer? Why or why not?

Are you satisfied with your experiences with corporate prayer in your church? Why or why not?

STIR IT UP

If you've ever taken the lid off an old can of paint, you know it's not useable right away. When paint sits for a while, different components can separate and settle out. Sometimes the paint congeals into clumps, and often you'll find a slimy skin covering the liquid.

For the paint to be useable again, it must be stirred up. That's why they give you that little wooden stick when you buy a new can of paint from the store: so that you can stir up the contents when they get old and make the colors vibrant and useful once again.

In Today's Scripture Focus, Jeremiah 33:2-3, we see God stirring up Jeremiah to a renewed focus on and prioritization of prayer.

> *Thus says the LORD who made the earth, the LORD who formed it*
> *to establish it—the LORD is his name: Call to me and I will answer you,*
> *and will tell you great and hidden things that you have not known.*

That's verses 2-3. If we look back at verse 1, we'll start to see why Jeremiah needed to be stirred up: "The word of the LORD came to Jeremiah a second time, while he was still shut up in the court of the guard." God's prophet had been taken prisoner by the religious officials in Jerusalem. But that wasn't the worst of it. During the time of Jeremiah's captivity, Nebuchadnezzar and the Babylonians had laid siege to the city of Jerusalem and were close to conquering God's people.

In other words, Jeremiah was in the middle of a dark time. And God responded by inviting him to pray.

What obstacles regularly prevent you from maintaining a healthy, consistent life of prayer? Record three.

1.

2.

3.

What people, experiences, or events has God used in the past to stir you to pray?

GOD'S NAME

The first words of Today's Scripture Focus are "Thus says the LORD" (v. 2). That's an important sentence, right? Those words should make anybody sit up and take notice. And just to make sure Jeremiah didn't miss who was addressing him, notice how the text continues: "Thus says the LORD who made the earth, the LORD who formed it to establish it—the LORD is his name" (v. 2).

I'll be the first to admit I'm not the sharpest knife in the drawer, but even I can figure out what's being emphasized in this verse: God was talking. The One who created everything in the universe with just a word from His mouth was about to speak. The One who sustains every person, every animal, every rock, every tree, and every molecule floating in space—He wanted to say something to you, so He said to listen up.

When have you been confronted by the power and authority of God? What happened?

But there's a twist in the way God announced Himself. The name He used was Yahweh: "Thus says Yahweh who made the earth." In most Bibles *Yahweh* is translated *LORD* in all capital letters.

This choice of names is important because Yahweh is God's covenant name. It's personal and close.

Read the following passages of Scripture in which God's personal name, Yahweh, is used. What do these verses teach you about Him?

Genesis 3:8-14

Exodus 3:13-15

Psalm 145:18-21

I have the opportunity to meet a lot of new people through our church and our radio ministry, and I can say for certain that I've never asked anyone to address me with any kind of formal title. I've never introduced myself as "Dr. MacDonald" or even "Pastor MacDonald." I've never said, "You can call me Reverend MacDonald."

That's because I'm interested in relationship. People who constantly reference their titles and honors are saying, "Don't forget who I am. Mind your p's and q's. Stay in your place." That's not what I want to communicate to the people I speak with, and that's not what God wanted to communicate to Jeremiah. God said, "Come talk to Me as Yahweh. I want to have a personal conversation with you."

God says the same thing to us. Yahweh is the name of God that's used most often in the Scriptures. More than 6,800 times the text identifies Him as Yahweh. Over and over again, God invites us to know Him personally. He says: "I want a relationship with you. I'm inviting you to make a covenant with Me."

What's your reaction to the previous statements? Why?

How do you picture God in your mind when you pray?

Do you see how amazing this invitation must have been for Jeremiah? That the Creator of the universe wanted to speak with him informally? But that's not even the craziest part of Today's Scripture Focus.

GOD'S OFFER

Not only did God invite Jeremiah to speak with Him personally on a relational level, but He also made Jeremiah an offer of assistance. He said, "Call to me" (Jer. 33:3).

Remember, this was a troubling time for everyone. Jeremiah was in prison, and a fearsome army was threatening the entire nation of Israel. In the middle of that mess, God got in touch with Jeremiah and said, "Call to Me." And God is saying the same thing to us through this text. When things are rough and we don't know how to get out of the mess we're in, God says, "Call to Me."

That's prayer.

Do you find it easy or difficult to call to God in times of trouble?

Do you find it easy or difficult to call to God when things are going well?

What are you experiencing in life for which you need God's help? Have you cried out to God about it?

Try to imagine for a moment that you don't know what prayer is. Pretend you've never heard of prayer before, and I said, "You have the opportunity to talk to the Creator of the universe, and He will listen to you. Not only that, but He also wants you to talk with Him; He's asked you to call on Him whenever you wish." How would you respond? You'd shout, "Yes!" You'd say, "I need to take advantage of this opportunity *right now!*"

God's offer of assistance is staggering. The idea that prayer exists is staggering. But so many of us treat that opportunity disdainfully because we've become so accustomed it. Our familiarity with prayer has bred contempt.

If someone deeply appreciated being given the opportunity to speak regularly and continually with God, how would they behave?

Do you behave that way? Why or why not?

Let's make one more clarification before we wrap up for today. God said, "Call to Me." He didn't say, "Ask Me, and I'll give you what you want." God's offer of assistance isn't a guarantee that He will fix whatever has gone wrong in our lives or extricate us from any mess we stumble into.

No, God offers Himself. He says, "Call to Me," and once we cry out to Him, we let Him decide what needs to happen. That's prayer.

THE RESULT IS FRAGRANT

TODAY'S SCRIPTURE FOCUS >

"Offer to God a sacrifice of thanksgiving,

and perform your vows to the Most High,

and call upon me in the day of trouble;

I will deliver you, and you shall glorify me." Psalm 50:14-15

If you have children or if you've been around children for any significant period of time, you know they're not shy about vocalizing their needs and desires. And the more intensely they feel something—fear, hunger, happiness, and so on—the more intensely they express that feeling to those around them.

Any parent can remember the days of being awakened in the middle of the night by the cries of their child: "Mommy!" "Daddy!" I can remember times when my wife and I would be startled out of sleep by the sound of our kids' little fists pounding on the bedroom door because they had a need, and their need drove them to seek those who could meet it, no matter the cost.

When children are scared in the middle of the night, they call out. When they're lost and alone and need direction, they call out. When they're hurt and need a parent to help them or heal them, they call out. They don't wait or worry about interrupting. They verbalize their need, and they usually verbalize it with intensity.

We can learn a lot from children when it comes to prayer. Because no matter how old we are or how much we grow, we're always children in relation to God. We never get beyond the point where we no longer need to call to Him.

In your mind what does calling out to God look like?

In what circumstances do you typically call out to Him?

TAKING IT UP A NOTCH

Yesterday we looked at Jeremiah 33:3, in which God offered assistance to the prophet Jeremiah: "Call to me." We see the same word in Today's Scripture Focus:

> *Offer to God a sacrifice of thanksgiving,*
> *and perform your vows to the Most High,*
> *and call upon me in the day of trouble;*
> *I will deliver you, and you shall glorify me.* Psalm 50:14-15

We should pay attention to that word *call*. It's not a bland, everyday kind of word. It's an expression of urgency, intensity, and fervency. It's an invitation to cry out to God in a way that's shameless, loud, and intimate: "Call to Me." "Call on Me."

James 5:16 says, "The effective, fervent prayer of a righteous man avails much" (NKJV). And that's just the tip of the iceberg. It's amazing how many times in Scripture we're told to call out to the Lord—to cry out and lift our voices.

For example, look at Exodus 2:23-25:

> *During those many days the king of Egypt died, and the people*
> *of Israel groaned because of their slavery and cried out for help.*
> *Their cry for rescue from slavery came up to God. And God heard*
> *their groaning, and God remembered his covenant with Abraham,*
> *with Isaac, and with Jacob. God saw the people of Israel—and God knew.*

Circle any words and phrases in the previous verses that connect with the idea of crying out and being heard by God.

Read the following passages of Scripture and record what they communicate about intensity and fervency in prayer.

Isaiah 40:9

Psalm 116:1-4

Luke 22:39-46

Colossians 4:12

In spite of the testimony of Scripture, how often do we pray loudly? I'm talking about speaking to God out loud with significant volume. Is it true in your life that most of your prayers would be inaudible to a person standing beside you? How did we come to connect prayer with thinking, musing, and whispering—practices that are far from what the Bible portrays as prayer that God delights to answer?

How did you answer those questions as you read them?

God isn't particularly moved by our meditative whispering. Rather, He frequently invites us in His Word to cry out, to call out, to lift up our voices, and to pour out our hearts.

I remember witnessing that kind of genuine intensity and fervency in prayer when our family visited my grandmother. Sitting by her second-floor bay window in chairs that faced each other, she insisted on praying personally for me every time I visited. Taking my hand, she would lean forward, pausing at length to gather her sense of God's listening before she began. Starting with heartfelt adoration, she would praise and thank God at length before any specific petitions. She prayed for the kind of things that made me very uncomfortable: for God to crush my pride, to reinforce my total dependency, to protect me from temptation given my "great weakness," and so on.

I confess to never closing my eyes as she prayed for me, because I was spellbound by the experience of watching Grandma Eileen pray. She had lost one eye as a result of a bee sting when she was a child, and the dead eye had never been corrected cosmetically. Her prayers would build to a fever pitch. As her fervency grew, she cried out to the Lord with the closed eye streaming tears while the other eye looked lifelessly ahead. It was a scene that usually resembled *The Shining* more than an afternoon with Corrie ten Boom, but she modeled a passion in prayer that most people can't imagine.

With all my heart I believe I will get to heaven one day and learn that any good accomplished through my life was 100 percent in response to the prayers of Grandma Eileen and a number of other fervent pray-ers God has graciously placed in my path.

Do you demonstrate intensity and fervency when you pray? In what ways?

Who prays for you with genuine intensity and fervency?

OUT ON A LIMB

If you're starting to get really uncomfortable as you read this, bear with me. I realize the way God wired you may not easily lend itself to volume or intensity in prayer. You may not be called to lead multitudes of people to publicly and boldly "draw near to the throne of grace" (Heb. 4:16). I get that.

But that doesn't mean you can't max out your capacity for fervency based on the way God made you. All of us should express intensity and fervency in our prayers based on the ways we naturally express intensity and fervency in other areas of life.

What are you most passionate about in life? When do you get most excited?

How do you typically express that excitement and passion?

What would it look like to express intensity in prayer the same way?

Having said that, what we see taught about praying and prayer in the Bible never suggests that God says, "Whisper something to Me in passing; I know you're busy. Just throw a couple of thoughts in My direction, a couple of quick requests over your shoulder while you're on your way to the grocery store. That's all I desire."

Instead, I believe God's words on prayer are better summarized this way: "How much does this matter to you? If you'd turn your intensity dial to *full,* I'd like to meet you at the place where you express your heart fully."

Something wonderful happens in the heart of God when His children get themselves out on a limb and say from the depth of their souls, "God, if it's not You, it's nothing. We don't have another plan. We don't have another hope. All of our eggs are in Your basket; there's no plan B. We believe this is Your will as revealed in Your Word, and we're going to keep calling out with intensity and fervency until You act on our behalf."

Weak, timid prayers have no place in vertical church, and it's my sincere hope that they will have no place in your life and experiences with God.

Try praying today with renewed fervency about something that's on your heart.

INSURANCE

"I have spoken, and I will bring it to pass;

I have purposed, and I will do it." Isaiah 46:11

By the time Harvest Bible Chapel was 13 years old, we were maxed out in terms of worship space. We had no room for people or parking or more services in the converted warehouse we called home. The only way to continue reaching people was to find another building and relocate. But population density in the O'Hare corridor limited our options to a single property owned by the Catholic Church, and they don't sell often, especially not to an evangelical church. Nevertheless, our church's history is one of multiplied miraculous answers to prayer, so we began afresh to test the promises of God.

I filled my heart with faith based on Jesus' words in Mark 11:24: "Whatever you ask in prayer, believe that you have received it, and it will be yours." I frequently drove to the property to walk and pray. Our elders gathered on the vacant Catholic land, holding hands in a circle and calling out to God by faith, claiming the land for His glory and for the gospel. We strove with our prayers. We called out to God with intensity and fervency.

But we didn't get the property. We didn't receive what we asked for, and the experience was devastating for me. It was the first time I'd ever prayed in faith for something good without seeing God answer in the affirmative, and it left me confused and a little frustrated.

If you've had a similar experience—if you've been unsure whether you're prayers were accomplishing anything or whether God even heard them—keep reading. Because today we're going to explore three words that should help ease our fears and calm our frustrations: "I will answer you" (Jer. 33:3).

When have you prayed for something you desperately wanted but ultimately didn't receive? Record three instances from recent years.

1.

2.

3.

What emotions did you experience at the time these events occurred?

What emotions do you experience when you think about them now? Why?

YES AND NO

I believe God answers every prayer. Every one. And the reason I believe that is because God expressed that reality to us in His Word.

Today's Scripture Focus makes it clear that God is able to do what He wants to do:

> *I have spoken, and I will bring it to pass;*
> *I have purposed, and I will do it.* Isaiah 46:11

Yesterday we looked at Psalm 50:15, in which God said, "Call upon me in the day of trouble; I will deliver you, and you shall glorify me." Notice the certainty of those words. The day before yesterday we looked at Jeremiah 33:3, in which God said, "Call to me and I will answer you."

What's your reaction to God's promises in the three previous verses? Why?

"I will answer you." Those four words are insurance for us. God is able to answer our prayers, and He has promised to do so. How incredible! Of course, the next question is, What are the answers He gives to our prayers? There are three.

The first answer is yes. I believe this is the most common answer God gives when we call out to Him with fervency and intensity—and when we ask for things that align with His will:

> *This is the confidence that we have toward him, that if we ask anything according*
> *to his will he hears us. And if we know that he hears us in whatever we ask, we*
> *know that we have the requests that we have asked of him.* 1 John 5:14-15

I've never asked God for strength without receiving it. Not once. I've never asked God for wisdom without receiving it. Now, I've certainly made decisions that I later regretted and *wished* I'd prayed for wisdom, but I've never made that request without receiving help from God. It's the same for peace. Every time I've knelt down, presented my burdens to God, and asked for peace, He's generously granted my request.

When has God recently answered yes to your prayers? Record three recent experiences.

1.

2.

3.

How do you respond emotionally when God says yes to your prayers?

How can we determine whether our requests line up with God's will?

The second way God answers our prayers is by saying no. We need to get this in our minds, and we need to be OK with it. Sometimes God says no.

There are times when God says no because of us—when we pray for stupid stuff, for example. James 4:2-3 says, "You do not have, because you do not ask. You ask and do not receive, because you ask wrongly, to spend it on your passions." Other times we pray for good stuff, but we put a timeline on it. I don't know about you, but I've found God to be very unmoved by my ultimatums.

When have you prayed for something because of "your passions" (v. 3) rather than God's will? What happened?

There are also times when God says no to our prayers simply because He knows what's going on and we don't. Maybe He understands that what we consider good would actually be harmful. Or maybe He has something totally different in mind—something we have no way to think through or plan for.

As an example, I mentioned earlier how the elders of our church and I fervently and passionately prayed for the ability to purchase a vacant property owned by the Catholic Church. But we didn't receive what we asked for. God said no. I was confounded at the time because I didn't understand what God had in mind. However, just a short time later we were blessed to receive an 85-acre property that included a 285,000-square-foot building on a major four-lane road west of Elgin, Illinois, with a nine-hundred-car parking garage. It was purchased and built in 1993 at a cost of $53 million and given to our church for $1.

One more thing, and this is tough: sometimes God says no to our prayers because He has a purpose for the mess we're currently experiencing. That happened to Paul when he prayed that God would remove his thorn in the flesh.

Read 2 Corinthians 12:7-9. Are you willing to endure trials if God wants you to? Why or why not?

How should we react when God says no to our prayers? Why?

How do you react when God says no to your prayers?

WAIT

The third way God answers our prayers is often the hardest one for us to hear: wait. Sometimes God tells us to wait before we receive what we need. The good thing about this answer is that God basically says yes. The bad thing about this answer is that He inserts a period of time between our request and its fulfillment, and we never know how long that period of time will last.

Waiting isn't easy. Delays make us feel helpless—unless we focus on the promise rather than the timing. Jesus said, "Whatever you ask in prayer, you will receive, if you have faith" (Matt. 21:22).

So as you wait, believe you've received what you're asking for. That agonizing request cried out to God that's still hanging out there, that deliberate petition based squarely on a promise of God, those passionate longings to see people come to know Christ—believe you've received them. Instead of asking, "When will it come?" ask, "How will it be when it comes?" In faith, focus on the answer rather than the delay.

One more thing: be persistent as you wait. I'm convinced that many of us abandon our requests far too quickly because we lose faith.

Read Luke 18:1-8. What do these verses teach us about prayer? What do they teach us about faith?

What prayers are you currently waiting for God to answer?

How can you demonstrate persistence and faith in those prayers?

God will answer your prayers. That's your insurance policy. You can rest assured He will come through. Therefore, as you call out to God according to His will, pray with intensity. Pray with fervency. Pray with persistence. And pray with faith.

INSPIRATION

TODAY'S SCRIPTURE FOCUS   >

"May the God of hope fill you with all joy and peace in believing, so that by the power of the Holy Spirit you may abound in hope." Romans 15:13

As I look back over the many experiences of my life, I can see different ways God prepared me to move into the deeper waters of prayer. For example, complications surrounding the birth of our second son, Landon, forced my wife and me to grapple with the inspiring and terrifying realm of miracles on earth.

I remember thinking Landon looked a little blue as he entered this world, but the hospital staff quickly got him breathing and crying, and we wept for joy at the sight of our second son. After all the excitement I went home to get some sleep. Imagine my shock when I returned to the hospital and found my wife dressed and packed, sitting on the bed crying. "They've taken Landon by ambulance to Lutheran General's neonatal intensive-care unit," she said. She said he was turning blue and couldn't breathe; they were going to find the problem and "do what they could."

Do what they could? Every pastor who visits the hospital knows what those words mean, and it's never good. As the minutes turned to hours, the diagnosis was firm and grim: diaphragmatic hernia. It's a rare condition that occurs when the diaphragm doesn't close during gestation to keep the intestines below the stomach. Floating upward, the intestines force the heart to the right of the chest, compressing and preventing the lungs from proper growth. On Landon's X-rays we could see that his left lung was almost nonexistent, and his right lung was far below capacity.

When we saw Landon next, he was lying in a plastic tray under a heat lamp. We were told that 88 percent of children born with this condition don't survive their first 24 hours. We struggled to accept the nurses' verdict that our child might not live through the night.

What have been some dark moments in your life?

How did prayer impact those moments?

To this day I could take you to the parking space where Kathy and I bowed and prayed in a different way than we'd every experienced. We cried out to the Lord for Landon's life to be spared and for God to heal him and use him. And to our great joy, God answered our prayer in a way more generous and inspiring than we even dared to hope.

Landon was healed. It happened quickly and was irrefutably a miracle. I was there when the surgeon who sewed his internal organs in place looked at the post-operative X-ray. I saw the confusion and shock the doctor felt when he saw the heart back in its proper place and the squiggly lines across the X-ray revealing two perfectly healthy lungs. Landon was home in eight days, he required no follow-up surgeries, and he never dealt with that issue again.

I'm still inspired by that story! It fires up something inside me to hear about the powerful things God does when we approach Him with fervent, faith-filled, persistent prayer.

> **When have you witnessed or heard about God miraculously answering the prayers of His people? How did you respond?**

GREAT THINGS

We've been digging deeply into one of my favorite passages in the Old Testament:

> *Thus says the LORD who made the earth, the LORD who formed it to establish it—the LORD is his name: Call to me and I will answer you, and will tell you great and hidden things that you have not known.* Jeremiah 33:2-3

We've highlighted the invitation contained in verse 3: "Call to me." We've discussed the intensity we should bring in our response to that invitation—that our prayers should be fervent and persistent. We've seen the insurance policy granted to us in the next four words of verse 3: "I will answer you."

Let's focus now on the rest of that verse: "and will tell you great and hidden things that you have not known." God said, "I will answer you," but we want to know how He will answer. What will the answer look like? It's going to fit into two categories.

1. God will tell us hidden things. He promises to illuminate truths and realities for us that are hidden to other people, which is what we'll explore tomorrow.
2. God will tell us great things that will inspire us in our walk with Him. That's what we're exploring today.

Generally speaking, what makes you feel inspired and/or emotionally uplifted? Why?

How do you respond when you feel inspired? What actions do you take?

The more we get to know God through prayer, the more He will tell us great things about Himself and His work in the world. He will teach us about His love, for example. He will teach us about His faithfulness. He will show us the way His glory is demonstrated in creation. He will reveal the way His justice is displayed in our thirst for justice in the community.

Similarly, the more we bring our requests to God and ask Him to work in the world, the more inspired we'll become as He does "far more abundantly than all that we ask or think" (Eph. 3:20). He will tell us great things through His great actions—from the mundane to the miraculous.

In other words, He will grant us what Paul asked for in Today's Scripture Focus: "May the God of hope fill you with all joy and peace in believing, so that by the power of the Holy Spirit you may abound in hope" (Rom. 15:13).

What have you learned about God's character in recent months?

What do you find inspiring about His character?

How have you been inspired by God's work in the church? In your life?

THREE OBSTACLES

We need to understand that our inspiration is predicated on prayer. God inspires us by telling us great things, but we must initiate that conversation through prayer—by calling on God.

So let's finish today by exploring three obstacles that regularly and consistently keep followers of Jesus from praying as they should.

Anger. When we're angry, we don't pray—or maybe we become angry because we didn't pray. Anger causes us to say, "My situation shouldn't be like this; I won't accept these circumstances; I'm not good with it." We don't direct these words at God; that would be prayer. Rather, we stew in our own juices and engage in an internal dialogue that produces nothing but bitterness.

Read James 1:19-21. What do these verses teach us about anger?

How has anger affected your prayer life in recent months?

Fear. Fear is often a natural and good response. If I see a large bear in the woods, I should become afraid and run away. That's a positive response. But fear of danger, whether the danger is real or imagined, can cause me to ask questions that derail prayer: *Will God really come through? What if I can't find a way out of this situation? How can I do what God commands without taking any risks?*

If we allow fear to push us toward these questions and away from prayer, we'll simply remain afraid. Rather than casting all our cares on Him because He cares for us (see 1 Pet. 5:7), we'll cower in fear and helplessness.

Read 2 Timothy 1:6-14. What do these verses teach about fear?

How has fear affected your prayer life in recent months?

Doubt. Doubt occurs when we question the character and/or reality of God: *Is God really good? Am I sure He hears my prayers? Is He even real?* I vividly remember my times of doubt—and we all have them. We're all prone to unbelief and mistrust. But meditating on doubt is a powerful enemy of prayer.

Read James 1:5-8. What do these verses teach us about doubt?

How has doubt affected your prayer life in recent months?

It's somewhat ironic that prayer is the solution to the obstacles that block our desire to pray. We need to cultivate enough self-awareness to be able to step back and recognize, *I'm being motivated by anger right now.* Or fear. Or doubt. And when we make that realization, we must throw ourselves at God's feet in fervent prayer and allow Him to lovingly step in and inspire us with great things we "have not known" (Jer. 33:3).

Day 5 /

ILLUMINATION

"The secret things belong to the LORD our God, but the things that are revealed belong to us and to our children forever, that we may do all the words of this law." Deuteronomy 29:29

Life's filled with all kinds of moments. Some of them are big and loud, like fireworks on the Fourth of July. Others are intimate and quiet, like a dad watching his child play with sparklers for the first time in the backyard.

The same is true of prayer. Sometimes prayer is exciting and inspirational. God often answers prayers in ways that create a public witness to His greatness. He heals people. He brings families back together. He comes down in glory during times of public worship and leaves no doubt about the power of His manifest presence. Those are Fourth of July moments—the times of inspiration we talked about yesterday in which God tells us great things.

When have you experienced exciting, inspirational times of prayer?

God also uses the prayers of His people to meet with us quietly and intimately, like a father with his child. Sometimes He whispers only to us and tells us secret things about who we are, what we need, and where we're going. These are moments of illumination, and they're the subject of today's study.

HIDDEN THINGS

Today we're wrapping up our exploration of Jeremiah 33:2-3:

> *Thus says the LORD who made the earth, the LORD who formed it to establish it—the LORD is his name: Call to me and I will answer you, and will tell you great and hidden things that you have not known.*

Let's explore this idea of "hidden things that you have not known." Some Bible translations say "mighty things." The NIV says "unsearchable things." The Hebrew term that's been translated various ways is also used to describe fortified cities that were inaccessible and unassailable.

The point is that God knows things about our circumstances: great things, mighty things, hidden things. And this is one of the greatest blessings of prayer because God talks to us about these things. He tells us what we need to know. We're used to thinking about God speaking to us in and through His Word. But sometimes even His Word doesn't become clear until we quietly and prayerfully listen to what He has to say about it.

Unceasing prayer is a conversation in which we expect God to speak, and that's vital. Please do away with all forms of prayer that inform or instruct God without offering a moment of expectant silence during which we anticipate hearing from God.

When you pray, do you include specific times for listening to God? Why or why not?

When have you heard God share something specific with you during prayer? How did you respond?

Most Christians understand God is omniscient—that He knows everything—but we often think about His knowledge in general terms. He knows about molecules in space, He knows how many ants are currently living in the Amazon rainforest, He knows the deepest point of the Pacific Ocean, and so on. That's true; God knows these types of things.

But God's omniscience also applies to you and me on a very personal level. The Bible says, "Even the hairs of your head are all numbered" by God (Luke 12:7). Today's Scripture Focus says, "The secret things belong to the LORD our God, but the things that are revealed belong to us and to our children forever, that we may do all the words of this law" (Deut. 29:29).

Read the following passages and record what they teach about God's knowledge of our lives.

Psalm 139:1-6

Jeremiah 1:4-5

Ezekiel 11:5

What's your reaction to the idea that God knows every intimate detail about you? Why?

How has God shown you through your prayer life that He knows all about you?

Not only is God aware of the secret, intimate, and deeply buried details of your thoughts and actions—and the thoughts and actions of others—but He's also willing to share those details with you. He's promised to tell you "hidden things that you have not known" (Jer. 33:3).

PRAYER IS THE KEY

If you're wondering what those hidden things might be for your life, I can't answer that. I know what God has revealed to me, but the hidden things God would speak to you about are for you alone to know. Jesus said, "To the one who conquers I will give some of the hidden manna, and I will give him a white stone, with a new name written on the stone that no one knows except the one who receives it" (Rev. 2:17).

But I can tell you that prayer is the key for accessing those hidden things through regular, intimate conversations with God. You don't learn these things in college; you learn them through prayer. You won't learn these things in a small group or even at church; you discover them in prayer. You don't glean these things in books written by your favorite Bible teacher or scholar. You don't learn these things in experience or with the passage of time. You learn them in prayer.

What are the big questions troubling your soul right now? What do you long to know and understand?

How have you approached God with these questions so far?

Don't be satisfied with bland, boring prayer in which you close your eyes and try to say something interesting to God without falling asleep. Look to the Scriptures and discover the wonderful variety recommended for your times of prayer.

Follow the example of David, who wrote, "I wept and humbled my soul with fasting" (Ps. 69:10). Follow the example of Moses, who "lay prostrate before the LORD" for 40 days and nights (Deut. 9:25)—although you may want to start with an hour or two. Follow the example of Jesus, who "prayed more earnestly; and his sweat became like great drops of blood falling down to the ground" (Luke 22:44).

And follow the command of the apostle Paul, who told us to "pray without ceasing" (1 Thess. 5:17). Never end your conversation with God. Never feel that you're finished with prayer for the day and you're free to go off and do your own thing. Keep coming back to God throughout the day the same way you keep drawing air into your lungs.

> **Speaking practically, what does it mean to "pray without ceasing"? What steps can you take to maintain regular communication with God?**

> **When have you fasted as a form of prayer? What happened?**

> **What steps can you take to learn about different forms of prayer? What steps can you take to begin implementing those forms in your conversation with God?**

As we wrap up this week and finish our study together, I hope you'll see more and more that unceasing, fervent, faith-filled prayer is the key to a vertical church and a vertical walk with God. Prayer is the easiest thing to assume in church and the hardest thing to maintain. Prayer is the first thing our flesh discontinues when times get easy, and it's the last thing we resort to when times get tough.

I know from experience. Prayer has been the point of greatest victory in my walk with the Lord as well as the most persistent place of failure. I've prayed great prayers that shook the foundations of our church and led to an outpouring of God's glory. I've laid out before God, pleading for miracles in my life and family when they seemed impossible, only to receive them against all odds in answer to prayer. But I've also failed to pray and floundered as a leader and fallen into patterns of behavior that hurt the church, family, and myself.

> **What spiritual victories have you seen through prayer? What victories would you like to see for yourself, your family, and your church?**

In vertical church it all comes down to prayer. If you want to see a great outpouring of God's presence in your life and ministry, you must go much deeper into personal and corporate prayer. And please know I'm praying that you will.

Two Ways to Earn Credit
for Studying LifeWay Christian Resources Material

CHRISTIAN GROWTH STUDY PLAN

CONTACT INFORMATION:
Christian Growth Study Plan
One LifeWay Plaza, MSN 117
Nashville, TN 37234
CGSP info line 1-800-968-5519
www.lifeway.com/CGSP
To order resources 1-800-458-2772

Christian Growth Study Plan resources are available for course credit for personal growth and church leadership training.

Courses are designed as plans for personal spiritual growth and for training current and future church leaders. To receive credit, complete the book, material, or activity. Respond to the learning activities or attend group sessions, when applicable, and show your work to your pastor, staff member, or church leader. Then go to *www.lifeway.com/CGSP*, or call the toll-free number for instructions for receiving credit and your certificate of completion.

For information about studies in the Christian Growth Study Plan, refer to the current catalog online at the CGSP Web address. This program and certificate are free LifeWay services to you.

Need a CEU?

CONTACT INFORMATION:
CEU Coordinator
One LifeWay Plaza, MSN 150
Nashville, TN 37234
Info line 1-800-968-5519
www.lifeway.com/CEU

Receive Continuing Education Units (CEUs) when you complete group Bible studies by your favorite LifeWay authors.

Some studies are approved by the Association of Christian Schools International (ACSI) for CEU credits. Do you need to renew your Christian school teaching certificate? Gather a group of teachers or neighbors and complete one of the approved studies. Then go to *www.lifeway.com/CEU* to submit a request form or to find a list of ACSI-approved LifeWay studies and conferences. Book studies must be completed in a group setting. Online courses approved for ACSI credit are also noted on the course list. The administrative cost of each CEU certificate is only $10 per course.